# Discover!
# Social Studies

4

edovate
LEARNING CORP

Discover! Social Studies 4A

Published in Catasauqua, Pennsylvania by Discover Press, a division of Edovate Learning Corp.

334 2nd Street

Catasauqua, PA 18032

edovate.com

ISBN: 978-1-956330-09-0

Printed in United States of America

1st Edition

# Table of Contents

# Worktexts & Instructor Guides

## Worktexts

- Your Discover! course integrates all reading, writing, practice, ideas to extend learning, and opportunities for students to capture their ideas and connect learning to what matters to them.

- By providing both direct instruction and assessment opportunities, students are able to gain knowledge, reflect on what they learned, and apply it in both academic and real-world environments.

- To meet the needs of all learners, each worktext includes activities, instruction, and extensions that appeal to all learning styles.

- Each chapter is made up of lessons that connect to a central theme. Students have the opportunity to demonstrate understanding and think critically as they move through each lesson, and each chapter culminates with a student review, assessment, and opportunities for students to show what they know.

## Instructor Guides

- Each instructor guide is specifically constructed to complement the worktext, provide helpful suggestions for a home-based instructor, offer support, and broaden a student's knowledge base.

- Instruction and curriculum are differentiated with remediation, enrichment, assessment, and supporting activities suitable for a variety of learning styles.

- Answer keys for all activities are included in your instructor guide.

## Planning Your Day & School Year

- Each lesson takes approximately two to three days to complete, for a total of around 150 days of instruction through the school year. NOTE: Your worktext and instructor guide provide enrichment activities and discussion questions to take learning further and may add extra days to the school year. These are designed to inspire the instructor to customize the learning experience even further and encourage students to dive deeper into the topic.

- As you begin each lesson, we recommend completing three pages on the first day and two pages, including Show What You Know, on the second day.

- In the chapter reviews and assessment lessons, we recommend completing three pages on the first day and the remaining pages on the second day.

# Parts of a Lesson

## Lesson Overview (PAGE 1):

Each lesson opens with a list of goals or objectives designed to set the student up for success. Your instructor guide provides additional resources to reinforce concepts and add creativity to the lesson.

## Explore (PAGE 2):

This page is key, as it is designed to engage students and encourage the discovery of new concepts.

## Direct Instruction (PAGES 3–5):

In this section, the student gets to work by reading the content, capturing their own thoughts and ideas, and then practicing the concepts:

- **Read:** Students read informational text to gain knowledge about the lesson topic.
- **Write:** Students reflect on what they have read by creating a written response.
- **Practice:** Students practice what they have learned through various engaging activities, such as graphic organizers, matching, drawing, experiments, and hands-on learning.

## Show What You Know (PAGE 6):

This is where students demonstrate what they've learned by completing a carefully crafted assessment aligned with the lesson's objectives.

To reinforce learning, additional extension activities are included throughout each lesson:

- **Create:** Students are tasked with constructing a piece of art, such as a drawing, song, poem, model, etc., to demonstrate learning.
- **Take a Closer Look:** With these activities, students make observations about the world around them. In doing so, students are able to generate predictions, inferences, or conclusions based on those observations. In science, these are scientific investigations or STEM-based activities.
- **In the Real World:** These activities connect the lesson to real-world situations. Students get the opportunity to investigate or interact with real-world examples.
- **Online Connection:** Students use technology-based solutions to research and investigate concepts related to the lesson or create artifacts demonstrating their understanding.
- **Play:** In these activities, students create or play games related to the lesson, such as board games, card games, role-playing, etc.

# Chapter 1
## The New World

Hello, my dear friend! Monty the lion here!

A lot of lions are lazy and like to lay in the grass. But not me! I have always been very curious about the world.

So I wanted to see everything and learn everything. So, I decided to go to school and learn everything I can.

I grew up in South Africa. That is far far away in Africa. But now I am here in America. That's right! I'm not lyin'! Get it?

Do you want to hear how I came to your country? Let's roar through this!

Did you know that lions are kings of the jungle? Being a king means we have a lot of responsibility.

My father is old and ready to retire. And my brother, Marco, is younger than me. So I will soon have to take over as king.

But first, I need to get an education so that I can rule wisely. My father said the best school in the world is in America. So I went to Boston, to become the best leader I can be.

But I didn't want to go alone! I am very brave, because I am a lion. But I like hugs. A lot! So I took along my two favorite people to hug. My buddy, Leo, and my wife, Maria.

Do you want to hear what happened on my way there? Let's get to the mane story! Get it?

## What Will I Learn?

This chapter examines the history of colonialism in the United States. It looks at the settlements formed by early colonists, especially the Puritans.

## Lessons at a Glance

# Lesson 1

## The New World

**By the end of this lesson, you will be able to:**

- explain why Columbus wanted to find a new route to the Indies

- recognize that Columbus was in search of a new trade route when he landed in North America

- explain that Indigenous people lived in communities in North America before Columbus arrived

## Academic Vocabulary

Read the following vocabulary words and definitions. Look through the lesson. Can you find each vocabulary word? Underline the vocabulary word in your lesson. Write the page number of where you found each word in the blanks.

- **barter:** to trade fairly without using money (page ____)

- **indigenous:** originating in a particular region or country (page ____)

- **route:** a path taken to get from one place to another (page ____)

- **trade:** the action of exchanging something for something else (page ____)

**TAKE A CLOSER LOOK**

Look at the map. It shows what Europeans thought the world looked like in the 1400s.

What do you notice about the map? What do you wonder?

*World map by Martellus - Account of the Islands of the Mediterranean (1489), ff.68v-69 - BL Add MS 15760.jpg by Heinrich Hammer the German is in the public domain.*

# EXPLORE

Have you ever used a recipe that called for ginger, cinnamon, or pepper? These are all spices. Go on a scavenger hunt in your kitchen for spices. Make a list of the spices you see or the food that has spices in it. Ready, set, go!

...............................................

...............................................

...............................................

...............................................

Today, we can find these spices easily at the grocery store. But a few hundred years ago, they were hard to find. Spices come from plants, and most of those plants only grew in Asia. Europeans wanted these spices, but they didn't have many options for traveling across the world to get them. European explorers in the 1400s tried to find easy **routes,** or paths, to get spices and other foods from across the world. Why do you think Europeans were willing to travel so far to get spices?

## IN THE REAL WORLD

Here are a list of popular spices you might find in your kitchen:

- chili pepper
- cumin
- mustard seed
- nutmeg
- turmeric

Pick one of the spices. Look in a cookbook or online for a recipe that uses it.

# READ

## A Need for Trade

Today, we often **trade** a product, good, or service in exchange for money. For example, when you go to the toy store, you are trading your money for the toy you want.

Another method of trade is bartering. **Bartering** is an exchange of goods or services that involves making a fair deal without money. Can you think of an example of a time you may have bartered with a sibling or parent to trade something you had for something you wanted? Maybe you gave your brother your ham sandwich for his pudding cup.

In the 1400s, Europe traded and bartered their goods in exchange for goods they wanted (like spices) around the world. The problem was there was no easy way to get to eastern Asia from Europe.

## COLUMBUS'S MISSION

Christopher Columbus was interested in exploring and also wanted to be rich and famous. While some explorers searched for land routes traveling east from Europe, he believed it would be faster to sail west across the Atlantic Ocean.

Columbus convinced the king and queen of Spain to pay for his voyage. On August 3, 1492, Columbus and his crew set sail with three boats—the Niña, the Pinta, and the Santa Maria—in search of a new trade route. It's important to know that at this time, no one knew how large Earth was or that a huge piece of land existed between Europe and Asia.

On October 12th, Columbus and his crew spotted land. It was not in the Indies—the eastern islands of Asia—as they had expected. They were in a group of islands that are now called the Caribbean Islands.

# TAKE A CLOSER LOOK

This map shows the trips Christopher Columbus took. Find the red line. Trace the route Columbus sailed from Spain to the Caribbean Islands with your finger.

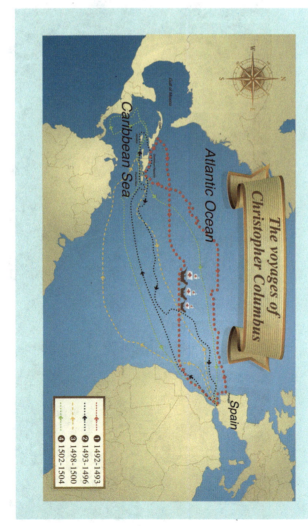

*The voyages of Christopher Columbus*

# READ

## Meeting Indigenous People

Christopher Columbus journaled about the wildlife, the plants, the weather, and the people he encountered. It is often said that Columbus discovered America, but people already lived there before he arrived. These people were **indigenous**, meaning they were native to the area. Since Columbus thought he landed on the shore of Asia in the Indies Mountains, he called them *Indians*.

The Indigenous people, who called themselves Taínos, were welcoming and eager to **trade**. They traded cotton and even parrots! Indigenous plants and animals were very different from those in Europe! The Taínos lived in communities on the Caribbean Islands now called Cuba, the Dominican Republic, Haiti, and Puerto Rico. Can you find these countries on the map? Point to them.

After several days of exploring, Columbus took his journal back to the king and queen of Spain so the people of Europe could know his findings! As Columbus shared about the New World, many people in Europe wanted to see the New World too! Soon, there would be many more explorations to this part of the world!

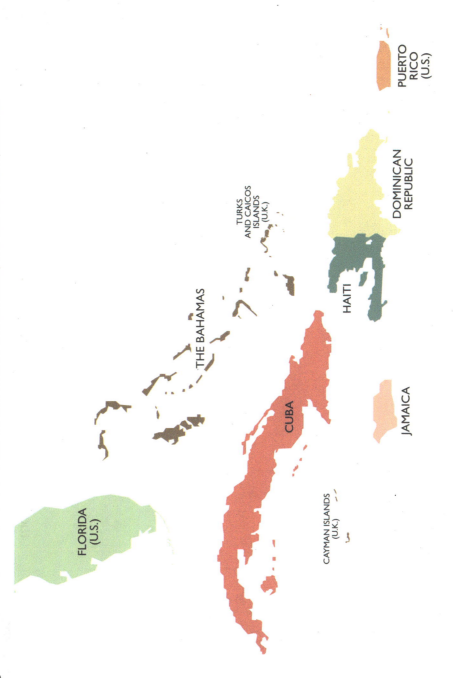

FLORIDA (U.S.)

THE BAHAMAS

TURKS AND CAICOS ISLANDS (U.K.)

CUBA

CAYMAN ISLANDS (U.K.)

JAMAICA

HAITI

DOMINICAN REPUBLIC

PUERTO RICO (U.S.)

# WRITE

Why did Christopher Columbus travel to the New World? What were his goals? What did he find?

_____

# PRACTICE

## Make a Trade

Imagine you and your parents are going to make a trade. Your parents are on one side of the house and you are on the other.

Make a map of your house below, and draw the trade route between you and your parents. What obstacles are along the way? What would stop you from making a straight line to get to the other side of the house?

Columbus thought he could find a straight route between Europe and Asia. Instead, he found the New World!

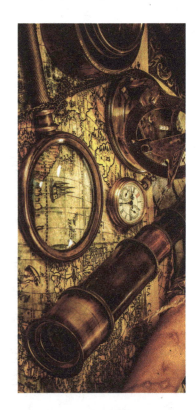

## REVIEW

In this lesson, you learned:

- Christopher Columbus wanted to find a new trade route to Asia to bring spices and other goods back to Spain.

- Christopher Columbus thought his ship landed in Asia. He was actually in the Caribbean Islands in North America, which he called the New World.

- In the New World, Columbus met Indigenous people who had always lived on the Caribbean Islands.

### Think About It

What was life like for the Indigenous people? What do you think their lives were like before Columbus arrived? How do you think the Indigenous peoples' lives changed after the Europeans arrival?

# SHOW WHAT YOU KNOW

1. What is it called to make a fair trade without using money?

   A. exchanging

   B. bartering

   C. native

2. What were Europeans, like Columbus, hoping to find and trade while exploring?

   A. journals

   B. maps

   C. spices

3. What is an Indigenous person?

   A. a person going on an exploration across the ocean

   B. a person native, or original, to a particular place

   C. someone who makes smart trades

4. Why did Columbus sail to the New World?

   A. to find a new trade route to Asia

   B. to trade with the Indigenous people in the Caribbean

   C. to prove the world was round

5. Do you think Christopher Columbus discovered America? Why or why not?

   .........................................................................................................................

   .........................................................................................................................

   .........................................................................................................................

## ONLINE CONNECTION

When Columbus arrived in the New World, he met Indigenous people who traded things like cotton and parrots. Use a computer to find out what other plants and animals are indigenous to the Caribbean Islands. List several of the plants and animals below.

..............................................

..............................................

..............................................

..............................................

# Lesson 2

## Jamestown

**By the end of this lesson, you will be able to:**

- describe why many European countries wanted to start colonies in North America
- find the following locations important to colonial times on a map: England, the New World (North America), the Atlantic Ocean, and Jamestown
- describe events that led to the creation of the Jamestown settlement

### Lesson Review

If you need to review exploration, please go to the previous lesson titled "The New World."

### Academic Vocabulary

Read the following vocabulary words and definitions. Look through the lesson. Can you find each vocabulary word? Underline the vocabulary word in your lesson. Write the page number of where you found each word in the blanks.

- **fertile:** moist and full of nutrients to help crops grow (page ___)
- **fort:** a small community protected by walls and watchtowers (page ___)
- **indentured servants:** settlers who agreed to help build a settlement without payment in exchange for a free trip to the New World (page ___)
- **malaria:** a disease commonly carried by mosquitoes in the 1600s (page ___)
- **plantation:** a large farm (page ___)

**CREATE**

In this lesson, you will learn about a settlement in the New World called Jamestown. This settlement was started in 1607. Let's start a timeline of events in American history. You can add to the timeline after each lesson. Put these events on your timeline to start.

- 1492 — Columbus found the New World as he searched for a trade route to Asia.
- 1607 — Jamestown was settled in Virginia.

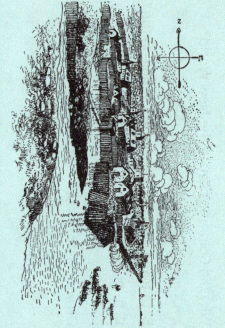

Illustration of Jamestown, 1622

# EXPLORE

Imagine you wanted to travel somewhere else today. Where would you go? How would you get there? Why would you want to go?

Use the table to draw or write your answers to each question.

| I would go... | I would get there by... | I want to go because... |
|---|---|---|
|  |  |  |

As you complete this lesson, think about how your answers compare to why people traveled to Jamestown and how they made the journey. Are there any similarities? Are there any differences?

# READ

## The New World

After Christopher Columbus landed in North America in 1492, he wrote detailed journal entries about the unique plants, animals, and people he encountered. Many Europeans from England read about his findings and wanted to come to the New World themselves.

Look at the map. Find England and the Atlantic Ocean, which separates England from the New World. Then find North America, which was considered the New World. Finally, find Jamestown on the map. Jamestown is located in modern-day Virginia and was the first permanent English settlement in North America.

On the map, draw the route people may have taken to get from England to Jamestown.

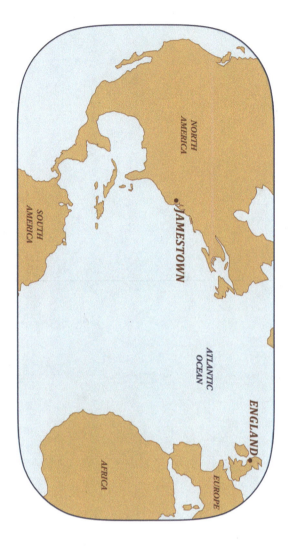

## Riches in the New World

Why did people want to come to the New World? Explorers wrote about a land where winters were mild and summer rain kept the soil fertile. **Fertile** soil was moist and full of nutrients that helped crops grow. Explorers also wrote about the woods, the fields, the different kinds of birds to eat, and the flowing rivers full of fish. Many people in Europe wanted the opportunity to have a better life with plenty of resources to farm, hunt, and fish. Some people in England also wanted to settle across the ocean because they believed there was gold in the ground that could make them rich.

# CREATE

Create a dough or clay map of the area where the Jamestown settlers would have traveled. Use the dough or clay to shape the continents of North America and Europe on a piece of cardboard, leaving space in-between to show the Atlantic Ocean. When the dough or clay is dry, paint the continents and label England, the New World, the Atlantic Ocean, and Jamestown.

# READ

## The Beginnings of Jamestown

In 1607, a man named John Smith guided a group of over 100 people to Jamestown from England. Several of the settlers were men looking for an adventure. Others just wanted to get rich and return to England. Many people in the group did not plan to build houses and plant crops.

After a long journey across the Atlantic Ocean, the group chose to build a fort on the James River. A **fort** is a community protected by walls and watchtowers. The settlers built their fort in an area a short distance from the ocean. They thought it would be a good place to hunt and fish near the James River while remaining hidden from ocean attacks and Indigenous people who may be angry about Europeans being on the land.

Unfortunately, the settlers soon found out the location of their new home had many disadvantages. Since the river was so close to the ocean, it was mostly saltwater. Men who drank it got sick. In addition, there were many mosquitoes carrying diseases like malaria. **Malaria** is a disease that can cause very high fevers and even death. Settlers in Jamestown also realized they did not know how to plant crops successfully. Also, the settlers found no gold.

Even though their location made settling difficult, John Smith knew settlers would have to work if they wanted to eat. Smith bartered with local Indigenous people. He traded tools like axes for corn and beans. Six months after their arrival, Smith returned to England. While he was gone, the settlers suffered a cold winter now known as "the Starving Time." During this winter, many settlers died.

Describe the advantages and disadvantages of settling near the James River.

.....................................................................

.....................................................................

.....................................................................

**A Reconstructed Fort in Jamestown**

# READ

## A New Plan

In 1609, a group called the Virginia Company who was dedicated to the success of Jamestown came up with an idea. They began sending settlers they knew would work hard in Jamestown. These **indentured servants** agreed to help build the settlement without payment in exchange for a free trip to the New World. It was not long after these servants began working on large fields called **plantations** that the success of the Jamestown colony increased. The servants became experts at growing crops that grew well in the South's fertile soil. One crop that grew very well was tobacco.

**Tobacco Plants**

## Leafy Gold

In the 1600s, no one knew the dangers of tobacco. Many people in Europe smoked it in pipes and cigars, and they were willing to pay a lot of money for it. In Jamestown, plantation owners knew it was valuable, and their goal was to grow as much as possible.

There was no gold in the New World, but tobacco became just as valuable. With the help of John Smith and the Virginia Company, many colonists who went to the New World to be rich were achieving that dream.

# TAKE A CLOSER LOOK

The local Indigenous people belonged to the Powhatan tribe. Chief Powhatan's daughter was Pocahontas. Have you heard of her? Pocahontas did not love John Smith, as you may have seen in a book or movie about her. Instead, she married a man named John Rolfe—a settler who was one of the first to realize tobacco would grow well near Jamestown.

*Pocahontas, age 21, 1616 by Ann Longmore-Etheridge is in the public domain.*

As more settlers and servants arrived from England to clear more land for plantations, they forced the Indigenous people to move. There were many disagreements between the two groups over land during this time.

# PRACTICE

Organize the events that led to the creation of the Jamestown settlement in order by rewriting each of these phrases in the boxes below.

_____ John Smith bartered with local Indigenous people to trade tools for food.

_____ Colonists set up a fort on the James River.

_____ The Virginia Company sent indentured servants to Jamestown.

_____ John Smith led men from England to the New World to start the colony of Jamestown.

_____ Many men got sick from drinking the river water, and some died of malaria.

_____ Colonists learned that tobacco grew well in Virginia and was worth a lot to Europeans.

| | |
|---|---|
| 1. | |
| 2. | |
| 3. | |
| 4. | |
| 5. | |
| 6. | |

# REVIEW

In this lesson, you learned:

- England and the New World (North America) are across the Atlantic Ocean from each other.

- Jamestown is located in present-day Virginia.

- Many European countries wanted to start colonies in North America for new land, new lives, and to become rich.

- Settlers in Jamestown suffered through a long, cold winter before their settlement was successful—not with gold, as they had originally thought, but with a crop called tobacco that was worth a lot of money.

## Think About It

How do you think the climate in Virginia and the southern colonies made plantations successful?

Look at the map and notice that there are letters over specific locations. Figure out what location each letter represents and write the correct letter on each line below.

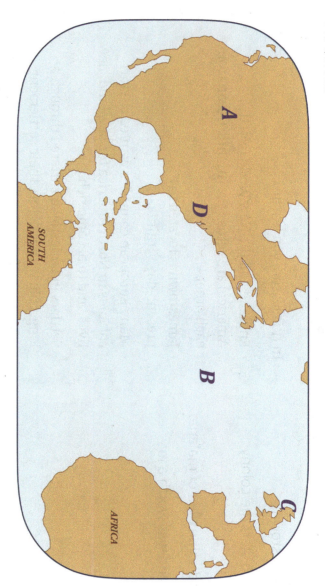

1. Which letter shows the location of North America? ___

2. Which letter shows the location of England? ___

3. Which letter shows the Atlantic Ocean? ___

4. Which letter shows the location of Jamestown, Virginia? ___

Circle the correct answer for each question.

5. Why did some Europeans want to settle in North America?

A. to have their own land

B. to start new lives

C. to be rich

D. all of the above

6. Why did most settlers in Jamestown choose to go to the New World?

A. to take land away from Indigenous people

B. to find gold and be rich

C. to start fishing businesses

D. to move to a more sophisticated land

7. What was the name of the time period during the first winter when many in Jamestown died?

A. the Starving Time

B. the Mayflower Compact

C. the Deep Freeze

D. the Coldest Winter

# SHOW WHAT YOU KNOW

Organize the events in order that led to the creation of the Jamestown settlement by arranging the lettered events in order on the timeline below.

**A.** John Smith returned to England. While he was gone, the settlers suffered a cold winter.

**B.** Settlers built a fort on the James River.

**C.** Jamestown became successful, not for gold but for the tobacco that grew well in the area.

**D.** A man named John Smith guided a group of people to Jamestown from England.

**E.** Settlers became sick from drinking water from the James River and got diseases from mosquitoes.

**F.** Indentured servants arrived in the New World and worked on large plantations.

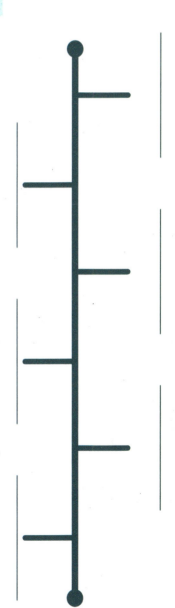

## ONLINE CONNECTION

Choose a person connected to the Jamestown settlement to learn more about:

- John Smith
- John Rolfe
- Pocahontas
- Chief Powhatan

Ask your instructor to help you find videos and other information online to help you learn more about them. Then create a multimedia presentation about them.

# Lesson 3

## Pilgrims

**By the end of this lesson, you will be able to:**

- describe ways the king of England controlled English churches and their members
- explain why the Pilgrims traveled to and settled in North America
- describe the challenges the Pilgrims had in Plymouth including why the first winter was very hard for the Pilgrims
- identify how Indigenous people helped the Pilgrims survive in America

## Academic Vocabulary

Read the following vocabulary words and definitions. Look through the lesson. Can you find each vocabulary word? Underline the vocabulary word in your lesson. Write the page number of where you found each word in the blanks.

- **harvest:** to gather crops after they have grown (page ___)
- **motivation:** a reason for acting or behaving in a particular way (page ___)
- **Pilgrims:** a group of people motivated to travel to the New World specifically for the freedom to practice religion the way they wanted (page ___)
- **separate:** to move apart from others; to form a different group (page ___)

**IN THE REAL WORLD**

Think about different forms of transportation that travel on water. There are canoes, speed boats, cruise ships, and many more.

Look at the images below of a boat and a ship. What are some differences you notice between boats and ships? If you were traveling across an ocean, which would you use? Why? Talk to your instructor about your answers.

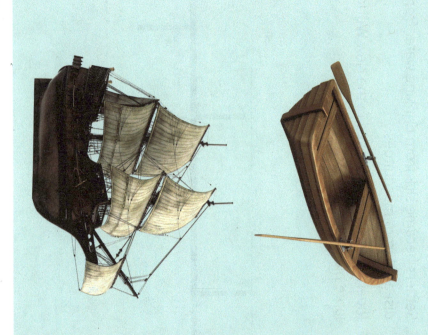

# EXPLORE

Have you ever thought about why people do the things they do? A **motivation** is a reason for acting or behaving in a particular way. Reasons for acting or behaving can come from a need that you have to fulfill, a strong desire, or because you were persuaded by someone else's actions or words.

Think about what motivated you to get out of bed this morning.

- Was it because of a need? Maybe you were hungry.
- A strong desire? Maybe the sun was shining and you couldn't wait to start the day.
- Were you persuaded by a parent or your alarm clock? Maybe it was time for school.

Now, think of a few things you recently did. What was your motivation for doing them? Fill out the chart below to show each thing you did and why you did it.

## TAKE A CLOSER LOOK

The Europeans were motivated to move to the New World even though they had to make a dangerous journey across the ocean. Why do you think Europeans were motivated to explore and settle in the New World? Write some of your ideas on the lines below.

What Motivates You?

| THING I DID | MY MOTIVATION |
| --- | --- |
|  |  |

# READ

## The Church of England

Do you remember learning about Columbus's voyage in 1492? His findings inspired many people to explore the New World and start new lives there for many different reasons. You may have heard about the group you are going to learn about today, but you may not know the whole story. A group of Christians in England, known as the **Pilgrims,** were motivated to travel to the New World specifically for the freedom to practice religion the way they wanted.

In the 1600s, the king of England required everyone living in the country to follow one religion and worship the same way. The king controlled English churches and their members by telling them what prayers to pray and how events in the Bible should be understood.

The Pilgrims didn't have the same beliefs as the king. They understood stories in the Bible differently. They wanted to worship like their families had before the king was the ruler of England. The Pilgrims tried to set up their own church services, even though they knew it was against the law. When the king found out, many were punished with prison or death.

The Pilgrims did not want to change their beliefs or live with the threat of prison or death. They decided their only option was to **separate** themselves from the Church of England by leaving the country. They called themselves Separatists. After hearing stories of the New World, the Pilgrims were motivated to move there so that they would no longer be controlled by the king's religious rules.

# TAKE A CLOSER LOOK

The star shows Plymouth on the map of Massachusetts. The Pilgrims chose this location because there was a large harbor for their ships, plenty of fertile land for planting crops, and a river nearby for fresh water. Can you think of other reasons early settlers would choose to live near a large body of water? Write your ideas on the lines below.

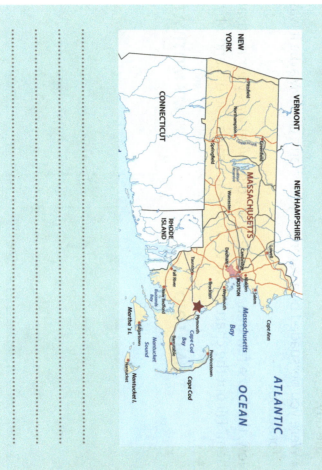

# READ

## A Long Voyage

In September 1620, about 100 Pilgrims left England on a large ship called the Mayflower. The voyage was long and difficult. The Pilgrims were crowded close together on the ship. For many days, the sea was very rough, and many people got sick. A big storm even blew them in the wrong direction! After more than two months at sea, the Pilgrims finally arrived in the New World. They meant to sail to Virginia, but they landed in present-day Plymouth, Massachusetts.

### THE FIRST WINTER

The Pilgrims quickly found that they were not prepared for life in the New World. The winter months were cold, and it was hard to plant crops in the frozen ground. They also struggled to find materials and to build homes. Many Pilgrims slept on the Mayflower through the winter, and almost half of them died before spring. The Pilgrims started to think they wouldn't be able to survive in the New World.

## ONLINE CONNECTION

Through the spring and summer, the Pilgrims learned a lot about how to survive in their new home due to a lot of help from the the Wampanoag—the Indigenous people of that area. After a successful fall harvest, they invited the Wampanoag people to a large feast. We now remember this as the first Thanksgiving.

Three crops that grew really well were squash, beans, and corn. The natives called these "the three sisters" because they helped each other grow when planted close together.

Use a search engine to find more information about "the three sisters." Talk about the information that you find with your instructor.

# WRITE

What motivated the Pilgrims to move to the New World? Write your thoughts on the lines below.

....................................................................

....................................................................

....................................................................

# READ

## HELP FROM THE INDIGENOUS PEOPLE

A group of Indigenous people from the Wampanoag tribe lived nearby. The Wampanoag, including one man named Squanto, watched the Pilgrims struggle through the first winter. Since Indigenous people had lived in the area for a long time and were familiar with the land, they decided to help. They taught the Pilgrims how to **harvest** crops. They also traded fur, food, and tools with the Pilgrims. Without their help, the Pilgrims may not have survived.

# PRACTICE

## Make a Comic

What challenges did the Pilgrims face during their first winter in Plymouth? How did they overcome these challenges?

Design a comic strip that illustrates the Pilgrims' arrival in the New World and how they survived their first year.

# REVIEW

In this lesson, you learned:

- The king of England controlled English churches and their members.

- The Pilgrims were motivated by religious freedom to travel to and settle in North America.

- The first winter was hard for the Pilgrims because they weren't prepared for the cold, and they couldn't plant crops in the frozen ground.

- Indigenous people in the Wampanoag tribe, who had lived in the area for a long time, helped the Pilgrims survive by teaching them how to harvest crops and by trading with them.

## Think About It

Think about the materials the Pilgrims would have needed to build shelters. Where might these materials have come from? Can you imagine why it was so hard to do this during winter?

# SHOW WHAT YOU KNOW

1. How did the king of England control the Church of England and its members? Circle all correct answers.

   A. He told people what types of prayers they could pray.

   B. He let people have their own types of church services.

   C. He threatened people with prison or death if they did not follow his rules.

   D. He told people how to interpret the Bible.

2. Read the causes below and draw a line to match each to its effect.

| CAUSE | EFFECT |
|---|---|
| The Pilgrims wanted freedom to practice their religion the way they wanted. | The Pilgrims could not plant crops and had few options for shelter. |
| The Pilgrims arrived in the New World during a very cold winter. | A group of Pilgrims decided to move so they could practice their religion without fear of prison or death. |
| The Wampanoag people were familiar with the land and how to grow crops. | The people helped the Pilgrims become successful at harvesting crops. |

3. How did the Wampanoag people help the Pilgrims? Circle all correct answers.

   A. They traded food and tools with the Pilgrims.

   B. They taught the Pilgrims how to build bigger ships.

   C. They taught the Pilgrims how to grow and harvest crops.

   D. They fought the king of England to let the Pilgrims practice their religion.

# CREATE

When the Pilgrims arrived in the New World, they didn't have houses. They had to build them from the materials that were available in the New World, like trees, rocks, and mud. What kinds of materials can you find around your home to build a model shelter? What kind of plan could you create to build a model shelter? Talk about your answers with your instructor and build your model!

4. What made the first winter in the New World so difficult for the Pilgrims?

........................................................

........................................................

........................................................

# Lesson 4

## Plymouth Colony

**By the end of this lesson, you will be able to:**

- identify the important agreement the government of Plymouth had in the colony
- describe why the Mayflower Compact was important to the Plymouth colony and the early formation of the country

### Lesson Review

If you need to review the Pilgrims' experience, please go to the lesson titled "Pilgrims."

......................................................

### Academic Vocabulary

Read the following vocabulary words and definitions. Look through the lesson. Can you find each vocabulary word? Underline the vocabulary word in your lesson. Write the page number of where you found each word in the blanks.

......................................................

- **colony:** a place in a different country where a group of people move to start new lives, but stay connected to their home country (page ___)

- **compact:** an important agreement between two or more people (page ___)

- **democracy:** a type of government ruled by the citizens (page ___)

- **Mayflower Compact:** a document signed by the Pilgrims on the *Mayflower* that described their government in the New World (page ___)

**IN THE REAL WORLD**

Have you ever made a special promise to anyone? Maybe you promised a sibling they could play a game with you or you agreed to take turns with a friend. How did the other person know you would keep your promise?

Another word for this type of promise is a contract. Ask your instructor what kind of important agreements, or contracts, they have signed. List them below.

......................................................

......................................................

......................................................

......................................................

# EXPLORE

Do you remember learning about the Pilgrims traveling to the New World from England in the last lesson? The Pilgrims were in an unfamiliar place far away from their king. Their first winter was really tough—they did not have many options for shelter or food. Many people crowded together on the *Mayflower* throughout the winter.

How do you think the Pilgrims got along together during those first few months? Do you think they had any disagreements?

Think about a time when you and a sibling or a friend had a disagreement. How did you solve the conflict? In the speech bubble below, write or draw an illustration of the disagreement. In the cloud, write or draw your solution.

**DISAGREEMENT**

**SOLUTION**

# TAKE A CLOSER LOOK

Different countries have different types of governments. In the United States, we have a democracy. A country has a democracy when its government is ruled by its citizens. Democracies do not have kings and queens who make all the laws on their own; they have elections where people vote for their leaders.

What do you know about America's government? How is it different from England's government where kings and queens rule? In government, how do people work out their disagreements? Think about these questions as you continue through this lesson.

# READ

## A New Land

When the Pilgrims arrived in the New World in 1620, they were in a new place by themselves. Can you imagine how they felt? Think about a time when you joined a new sports team or club where you were without your parents. How did you feel? You might have felt alone, excited, or nervous. Much like you, the Pilgrims felt excited but also nervous. They left Europe for religious freedom, but now they were on their own.

The Pilgrims called their new colony Plymouth. A **colony** is a place in a different country where a group of people move to start new lives but stay connected to their home country. The Pilgrims moved from England to the New World to live on their own, but they were still getting materials and money from England. This made their new home a colony! With the king so far away in England, the laws for the Pilgrims changed. The king owned the colony, but he could not really tell them how to live their lives from day to day. The Pilgrims had to come up with some of their own rules and laws to ensure the colony would be successful. Who would make decisions for the group? Who would make sure everyone did their part to help? On the *Mayflower*, a group of men sat down together to discuss these questions before they arrived in their new home.

# WRITE

What types of disagreements do you think the colonists had in Plymouth?

**This is a photo of Plymouth Rock, which is said to mark the spot the Pilgrims landed in the New World.**

**Visitors can also see a model of the Mayflower in Plymouth.**

# READ

## The Need for a Plan

The Pilgrims knew they would have to work together to be successful in the New World. They also knew they needed strong leaders to help plan for the future of their colony.

When a promise is written down and people sign their names, it can be called a compact. A **compact** is an important agreement between two or more people. The **Mayflower Compact** was an agreement signed by the Pilgrims on the *Mayflower*. It defined rules that the Pilgrims would follow in order to get along and make laws for themselves without the king. All of the Pilgrims followed the rules in the Mayflower Compact, and eventually their settlement was successful. Since the new laws were controlled by the Pilgrims instead of the king of England, we often hear the Mayflower Compact referred to as one of the first examples of democracy in America.

While the laws have changed since the days of the Pilgrims in 1620, the ideas of democracy are still a part of the US government today.

**Pilgrims signing the Mayflower Compact**

## ONLINE CONNECTION

The Mayflower Compact was signed by 41 men on the *Mayflower* before the Pilgrims stepped onto their new home. It says that the men promise to act in ways that are good for everyone and to make fair laws while they live in Plymouth. The men would also choose a leader—someone who they promised to obey.

The Pilgrims chose William Bradford as the leader of their colony. He was the leader in Plymouth for 30 years! With your instructor, use an online search engine to find out more about William Bradford. Then create a poster that illustrates interesting facts about him.

## WRITE

Describe the document that the Pilgrims used as their first form of government. Why was this document so important to the Plymouth colony?

# PRACTICE

A compact is an important agreement. In order to be successful, a compact must be good for everyone involved. Additionally, everyone must promise to follow the agreement. The signature is what makes it so important! When you sign your name to something, you should be proud of it!

Make a deal with a sibling or parent. Get creative! Write the details below, and do not forget to sign it! Then tell how your agreement is the same as and different from the Mayflower Compact.

**Our Deal**

...............................................................................................................

...............................................................................................................

...............................................................................................................

...............................................................................................................

...............................................................................................................

...............................................................................................................

**How is this the same as and different from the Mayflower Compact?**

...............................................................................................................

...............................................................................................................

...............................................................................................................

...............................................................................................................

...............................................................................................................

...............................................................................................................

...............................................................................................................

_____          _____
Signature                                        Signature

# REVIEW

In this lesson, you learned:

- The Mayflower Compact was a type of agreement that detailed how the government would work in Plymouth Colony. It was important because it set up a government that was run by the colonists themselves.

- Before they arrived, the Pilgrims signed the Mayflower Compact, promising to follow the rules and laws in it.

- The Mayflower Compact helped the Pilgrims work together and be successful in Plymouth. It was America's first example of democracy!

## Think About It

Think about what life was like for the Pilgrims in Plymouth Colony. Why do you think having the Mayflower Compact helped make the Pilgrims more successful?

# SHOW WHAT YOU KNOW

Use the words from the Word Bank to complete the sentences.

**Word Bank:** Mayflower   colony   democracy   compact

1. A _____ is an important agreement between two or more people.

2. Plymouth was a _____, meaning that it was officially ruled by another country with people from that country living on the land.

3. In a _____, citizens help make decisions about the government and its leaders.

4. The Pilgrims promised to follow the rules and laws they wrote in the _____ Compact.

Read each sentence. Circle whether it is True or False.

5. True or False  In a democracy, a king makes the rules and laws for a country.

6. True or False  *Compact* is another word for "contract" or "agreement."

7. True or False  The Mayflower Compact was the first example of democracy in the United States, and those democractic ideas are still present in our government today.

# CREATE

There are many songs about important people and times in history.

Write a song or poem about the Pilgrims and the Mayflower Compact. Can you make it rhyme? Then sing it to your family.

# Lesson 5

# Two Worlds Meet

## By the end of this lesson, you will be able to:

- describe how life was different for people who moved to North America
- state the meaning of the word *barter*
- explain how the Indigenous people used their natural surroundings to survive and barter
- compare and contrast how the Indigenous people and settlers viewed owning land
- compare and contrast the Pilgrims with the Indigenous people they encountered
- describe how the lives of the Indigenous people changed because of colonial settlements

## Lesson Review

If you need to review trading and bartering, please go to the lesson titled "The New World."

If you need to review Pilgrims, please go to the lesson titled "Pilgrims."

## Academic Vocabulary

Read the following vocabulary words and definitions. Look through the lesson. Can you find each vocabulary word? Underline the vocabulary word in your lesson. Write the page number of where you found each word in the blanks.

- **alliance:** an agreement between two groups to help each other (page ___)
- **barter:** to trade fairly without using money (page ___)
- **Columbian Exchange:** travel and trade of people, food, animals, and diseases between Europe and the New World (page ___)
- **resource:** materials that can be used by people to reach a goal (page ___)
- **settler:** a person who moves to live in a new country (page ___)
- **trade:** the action of exchanging something for something else (page ___)

## PLAY

Look at the image below. The two children are bartering, or trading, items. Ask a sibling or your instructor to barter with you. Gather some small toys or similar items, divide them up, and have fun trading them with each other. Afterward, discuss what made your trades fair.

# EXPLORE

When we compare two things, we find similarities and differences. Think about how you would compare yourself to a friend or family member. What differences do you have? What do you have in common?

One way to find the similarities and differences of two ideas or things is to use a Venn diagram.

On the line above one circle, write your name. On the line above the other circle, write the name of the person to whom you are comparing yourself. Write several unique things about yourself and the other person in the circles under your names. Finally, write a few things you have in common in the middle.

Stretch yourself to think about characteristics on the outside—traits you can see—as well as characteristics on the inside—traits you cannot see, including personality, fears, and strengths.

Just like you compared yourself and another person, we can compare the English settlers and the Indigenous people. Think about what you have learned about these groups in previous lessons. How are they the same? How are they different?

# READ

## Life for the Settlers

Do you remember learning about the Pilgrims? This group of **settlers** moved from England to the New World to start new lives with religious freedom. Life was hard when they arrived in Plymouth. There were no other Europeans in the area and no grocery stores or shops to buy materials. Can you imagine living in a place that didn't have anywhere to shop? How would you get food to eat or clothes to wear?

When the Pilgrims moved to the New World, they had to learn how to live off the land. This means that if they needed anything they did not bring from England, they would have to use the New World's natural resources to find or make it. They learned from local Indigenous people how to hunt and fish to get food to eat. Eventually, they learned how to plant and harvest crops. Life was different for Europeans when they moved to the New World.

Do you remember from previous lessons how difficult the first winter was for the Pilgrims? They may not have survived without the help of the local Indigenous people who taught them how to live off the land. The relationship between the Pilgrims and the Wampanoags became very important for both sides. Chief Massasoit of the Wampanoag tribe created an alliance with the Pilgrims. An **alliance** is an agreement between two groups to help each other. They agreed to make fair **trades** for things they needed, and they agreed not to fight each other for **resources** on the land.

**This statue of Chief Massasoit stands in Plymouth, Massachusetts.**

# TAKE A CLOSER LOOK

This is a photo of what the colony of Plymouth may have looked like when the Pilgrims lived there. Can you point out several examples of how they lived off the land? What types of natural resources are in this image? List the resources you see on the lines below. How are the Pilgrims using the natural resources to help them survive in the New World?

...........................................................

...........................................................

...........................................................

## Indigenous People in the New World

What is something familiar to you that you know well? Soccer? Video games? Chess? The Indigenous people in the New World were very familiar with the land and the natural resources in their area. Most Indigenous people in the New World in the 1600s were expert hunters and fishermen. They knew which crops would grow well and when to plant and harvest them. They knew how to use resources in nature to survive because they had always lived there.

Nature was very important to the Indigenous people because they used it for everything! Without stores or money, the Indigenous people used their natural surroundings to survive. They grew fruits and vegetables, and they caught and killed animals to eat. They used animal skin and fur for clothing and shelter. Sometimes, they **bartered** to get things they couldn't grow or make. Many times, the Indigenous people bartered with the Pilgrims to exchange things they had for things they wanted. For example, Pilgrims used metal pots to cook. The metal didn't come from nature, but if the Indigenous people thought it could help them, they might make a trade for something they had such as an animal to eat. Can you think of something else the Indigenous people might have wanted that they couldn't get from nature?

The Indigenous people loved the land they lived on. They believed that nature belonged to all people and that land should be shared. Europeans believed that land could be owned by individuals. The Pilgrims even put fences up around their homes!

The Pilgrims were different from the Indigenous people in many other ways. The Pilgrims sailed to the New World on a huge ship called the Mayflower, while the Indigenous people used small row boats in rivers near their homes to catch fish or to trade with nearby tribes. The Pilgrims also brought many metal tools from England and used them, while the Indigenous people used tools they made from nature, such as bows and arrows, to hunt. Look at the image above. What do you think each natural tool was made of and used for?

The Pilgrims and the Wampanoags also dressed differently from each other. Look closely at the image above. What types of clothing differences do you notice?

WRITE

In what ways were the Pilgrims and the Indigenous people different? Use a pen or highlighter to find evidence in the text and then write your answers on the lines.

# The Columbian Exchange

In the 1500s and 1600s, many Europeans traveled to the New World after hearing about Columbus's findings. They soon learned that each area had unique plants and animals unfamiliar to the other. Explorers and settlers bartered with people in the New World for things they wanted to have in Europe. This started a big system of trading foods and animals between Europe and the New World. This system is now called the **Columbian Exchange.** Look at the map to the right, which shows some of the things that were exchanged. What do you notice? What do you wonder?

Unfortunately, as people traveled between the two lands more frequently, germs and diseases were traded too. Point to words on the map that name the germs and diseases that were traded. Although the New World was introduced to new foods and animals, many Indigenous people died from European diseases while others were forced to move from their land to make room for new settlers.

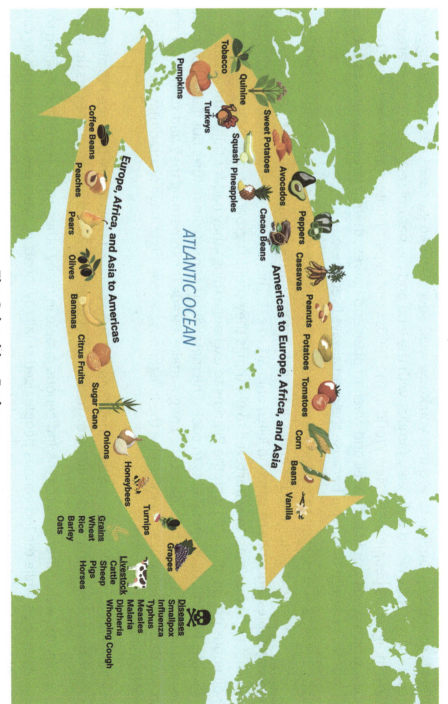

The Columbian Exchange

# PRACTICE

## Charting Trade

Use the map on the previous page to list items traded between Europe and the New World during the Columbian Exchange in the chart below. Talk about your answers with your instructor.

### FROM THE NEW WORLD TO EUROPE

### FROM EUROPE TO THE NEW WORLD

# REVIEW

In this lesson, you learned:

- Life was different for people who moved to North America.

- To barter means to trade fairly without using money.

- The Indigenous people used their natural surroundings to survive and barter.

- The Indigenous people had different views from the settlers about owning land.

- The Pilgrims were different from the Indigenous people they encountered.

- The lives of the Indigenous people changed because of colonial settlements.

### Think About It

In what ways do you live off the land? What foods or animals came to America during the Columbian Exchange that you are grateful for?

# SHOW WHAT YOU KNOW

Circle the correct answer(s) for each of the following questions.

**1.** The word *barter* means:

**A.** to give someone something you no longer want

**B.** to buy food or supplies at a store

**C.** to make a fair trade without using money

**2.** How did the Pilgrims think of owning land differently than the Indigenous people?

**A.** Pilgrims thought land should be shared, while the Indigenous people believed land was owned by individuals.

**B.** Pilgrims believed that land was owned by individuals, while the Indigenous people believed it should be shared.

**C.** Both groups believed land should be shared and not owned by individuals.

**3.** What did the Indigenous people use natural resources for?

**A.** They used resources from nature, such as animals, to survive and barter.

**B.** They used nature for farming with machines.

**C.** They didn't use nature much.

**4.** What was one major difference between the lifestyle of the Pilgrims and the Indigenous people?

**A.** The Pilgrims hunted for food, and the Indigenous people did not.

**B.** The Pilgrims used metal tools and big ships, and the Indigenous people only used what they could make from nature.

**C.** The Indigenous people didn't know how to live off the land, and the Pilgrims taught them.

# ONLINE CONNECTION

Use a computer to find out what natural resources were common in different areas of the New World. See if you can find some natural resources that these different areas had in common, including animals and plants. For example, one resource that many areas would have in common would be trees—a source of wood for building homes.

**5.** How did the lives of the Indigenous people change because of settlers moving to the New World and the Columbian Exchange?

**A.** Their lives improved and their populations increased.

**B.** Their lives may have improved for a short time, but they lost a lot of their land.

**C.** Their populations eventually decreased due to diseases being brought to the New World.

**6.** Describe how life was different for people who moved to North America.

...................................................

...................................................

...................................................

...................................................

...................................................

# Lesson 6

## Puritan Life

### By the end of this lesson, you will be able to:

- identify the reasons why the Puritans left England and went to the New World
- describe daily life in the Puritan communities
- compare and contrast the Massachusetts Bay Colony and the Plymouth Colony
- describe the laws the Puritans made

### Lesson Review

If you need to review the Pilgrims, please go to the lesson titled "Pilgrims."

If you need to review the Plymouth Colony, please go to the lesson titled "Plymouth Colony."

### Academic Vocabulary

Read the following vocabulary words and definitions. Look through the lesson. Can you find each vocabulary word? Underline the vocabulary word in your lesson. Write the page number of where you found each word in the blanks.

- **fine:** an amount of money paid as a punishment for breaking a rule or law (page ___ )
- **illegal:** against the law (page ___ )
- **purify:** to make something simpler or cleaner; to remove anything unnecessary (page ___ )

## TAKE A CLOSER LOOK

To purify means to make something simpler or cleaner or to remove anything unnecessary. This concept was important to the Puritans.

Look at the picture below. What do you think helps the water become purified? How might knowing the word *purify* help us know more about the beliefs and life of the Puritans? Talk about your thoughts with your instructor.

# EXPLORE

Did you know that it is against the law to use silly string in Connecticut? It is also a law that people cannot wrestle with bears in Alabama. Some laws that exist today seem really silly!

Ask your instructor to help you find other silly laws that exist or come up with a list of rules that do not make sense to you. Maybe you do not understand why you cannot wear a hat at the dinner table or why you can only cross the street on a crosswalk. Write a few on the lines below.

...............................................................

...............................................................

...............................................................

Based on what you know about the colonies, what laws do you think existed in colonial times that might seem strange today? In this lesson, you will learn about a group called the Puritans and the strict laws they had for their colony.

# CREATE

If you could come up with your own silly rule, what would it be? Maybe you would make everyone in your family touch their food to their noses before they put it in their mouth. How about requiring everyone to sing a song before bedtime? Create your own silly rule and write it below.

...............................................................

...............................................................

...............................................................

...............................................................

...............................................................

...............................................................

...............................................................

...............................................................

...............................................................

# READ

## Puritans Arrive in the New World

Do you remember the Pilgrims' motivation for coming to the New World? If you said it was for religious freedom, you are right! They did not like the Church of England, and they were not the only ones! In 1630, 10 years after the Pilgrims arrived on the *Mayflower*, the Puritans traveled to the New World. They were also motivated by religious freedom.

While the Pilgrims and Puritans both left England for religious freedom, they felt differently about the Church of England. The Pilgrims wanted to separate completely from the Church of England, but Puritans did not. Instead, the Puritans wanted to **purify** the Church's teachings by making it simpler and removing practices they believed were unnecessary. They wanted to live their lives precisely by the words in the Bible rather than participate in the traditions that were practiced among members of the Church of England.

## Massachusetts Bay Colony

The Puritans settled in Massachusetts Bay, which was not far from where the Pilgrims lived in Plymouth Colony. Massachusetts Bay is now called Boston. Look at the map to the right. Can you find Plymouth and Boston? Circle Plymouth in red, and circle Boston in green.

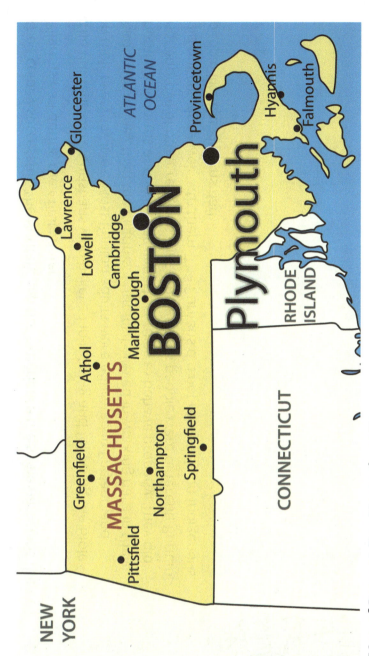

**Map of Present-Day Massachusetts**

# READ

## Daily Life for the Puritans

Do you remember how the Pilgrims struggled during their first winter? They could not find materials to build homes right away, and the ground was too cold to plant crops. Most Pilgrims slept on the *Mayflower* for months, and many died before spring.

Like the Pilgrims, the Puritans' new colony was also in Massachusetts; however, their experience arriving in the New World was very different. They had learned from the Pilgrims' struggles and came to the New World more prepared. The Puritans arrived before winter and had four ships of materials. They built homes faster and learned to grow food right away. They worked hard to make their colony successful. The Puritans did not experience the same hardships the Pilgrims had during their first winter.

The Puritans were Christians who believed in reading and following the Bible in their everyday lives. Most Puritan adults were educated in England and had more money than the Pilgrims. Puritans believed in working hard in their homes and farms and following very strict rules to behave properly. They did not approve of other religions. Since Indigenous people were different, Puritans did not get along well with them. The Puritans did not really rely on Indigenous people like the Pilgrims had.

## ONLINE CONNECTION

The Puritans' leader was John Winthrop. Ask your instructor to help you use a computer to find out more about him, and then write some facts about him on the lines below.

.........................................................

.........................................................

.........................................................

.........................................................

.........................................................

# READ

## Puritan Laws

The Puritans believed very strongly in their religion. All of their laws were based on the Bible. The Puritans did not have a democracy like the Pilgrims. The Puritans' church leaders were their government leaders. They were the only people who could make new laws in the colony. The laws the Puritans followed were very strict, and there were very serious punishments for breaking them. Take a look at some Puritan laws:

- People were not allowed to celebrate holidays.
- No one in the colony was allowed to practice a different religion.
- People were not allowed to miss church.
- Swearing or saying a bad word was **illegal**, or against the law.

Some people who broke the law were forced to leave the colony. Others had to endure harsh punishments or pay fines. A **fine** is an amount of money paid as a punishment for breaking a rule or law. Puritans made new, strict laws often.

**Puritan woman in the New World.**

## TAKE A CLOSER LOOK

For breaking a law, sometimes criminals spent time in the pillory. A pillory was a wooden frame with holes for the head and hands. Pillories were usually located outdoors in the middle of a busy area of the colony. Why do you think the Puritans used this form of punishment? Discuss your ideas with your instructor.

**Criminals put their heads and hands in the holes of a pillory as punishment.**

## WRITE

Describe daily life in the Puritan communities on the lines below.

...................................................

...................................................

...................................................

# PRACTICE

The Pilgrims and Puritans were similar in some ways but different in many others. Grab two different highlighters or colored pencils. Go back to the text and highlight their similarities in one color, and then highlight their differences in another. Use the details to fill in the table below. Don't forget to compare each group's reasons for moving to the New World and their colonies.

| PILGRIMS | BOTH | PURITANS |
| --- | --- | --- |
|  |  |  |

## REVIEW

In this lesson, you learned:

- The Puritans left England and went to the New World for religious freedom.

- They settled a colony called Massachusetts Bay, where they worked hard, practiced their religion, and followed strict laws.

- The Pilgrims and Puritans were similar and different in many ways.

**Think About It**
As people in England learned of the Pilgrims' and Puritans' colonies, what do you think happened to the population of Europeans in the New World?

# SHOW WHAT YOU KNOW

Think about what you've learned about the Puritans in this lesson. Read the statements on the left below and match it to the statement on the right that finishes the sentence.

**1.** _____ The king of England wanted all people to practice the teachings of the Church of England...

**2.** _____ The Puritans wanted freedom to practice their religion the way they wanted...

**3.** _____ The Puritans were well-prepared to live in the New World...

**4.** _____ The Puritans did not accept any religions other than their own....

**5.** _____ The Puritans were particular about how they lived their lives...

**6.** _____ The Puritans followed very strict laws forbidding holidays, bad words, and missing church...

**A.** ...so they did not starve or suffer as much as the Pilgrims did.

**B.** ...so they did not get along well with the Indigenous people in the area.

**C.** ...but a group of Puritans did not want to practice the king's religion in the same way.

**D.** ...such as reading the Bible and following its teachings every day. They worked hard and behaved properly.

**E.** ...and many were punished for breaking laws.

**F.** ...so they moved to the New World, where they could purify the Church and practice their religion freely.

**7.** How were the Puritans and Pilgrims the same? Circle all correct answers.

**A.** They both had a democracy.

**B.** They both came to the New World for religious freedom, even though their ideas of religious freedom were different.

**C.** They both did not get along well with the Indigenous people.

**D.** They both came from Europe to the New World.

**8.** How were the Puritans and Pilgrims different? Circle all correct answers.

**A.** The Pilgrims came to the New World to break away from the Church of England, and the Puritans just wanted to purify the Church's teachings.

**B.** The Pilgrims came from Spain, and the Puritans came from England.

**C.** The Pilgrims had a very hard time surviving in the New World at first, but the Puritans came better prepared for life in the New World.

**D.** The Pilgrims relied on the Indigenous people for help, but the Puritans did not.

# Colonization

## By the end of this lesson, you will be able to:

- identify the New England colonies, the Middle colonies, and the Southern colonies and locate them on a map
- describe the location of the Thirteen Colonies as being on the east coast
- identify important colonial leaders and people
- identify examples of common colonial jobs in the New England colonies, the Middle colonies, and the Southern colonies
- compare and contrast colonial life with how people live today

## Academic Vocabulary

Read the following vocabulary words and definitions. Look through the lesson. Can you find each vocabulary word? Underline the vocabulary word in your lesson. Write the page number of where you found each word in the blanks.

- **cash crops:** crops that grow well in an area and are worth a lot of money when sold (page ___)
- **coast:** the part of land that touches a large body of water, like an ocean (page ___)
- **colonist:** a person who settles in a colony (page ___)
- **colony:** a place in a different country where a group of people move to start new lives while staying connected to their home country (page ___)
- **founded:** started something (page ___)
- **region:** an area of land with unique characteristics (page ___)

Ask your instructor to help you draw a large map of the Thirteen Colonies on poster paper. Throughout the lesson, add information that you learn to your poster paper, including:

- The name of each colony
- The region in which each colony belongs, identified by color
- The location of big cities that exist today
- The land and climate of each region
- Jobs in each colony group
- Other characteristics you read about

# EXPLORE

Did you ever wonder what it was like to not have a refrigerator? How about a television? These are modern conveniences and were not always around. Modern conveniences include tools and machines we use today to make our lives easier.

Look at the list of modern conveniences and the year they were invented. Draw pictures illustrating how you think people may have done their jobs before these tools or machines existed.

| TOOL/ MACHINE | PURPOSE | YEAR INVENTED | ILLUSTRATION |
|---|---|---|---|
| Microwave | To heat food | 1946 | |
| Vacuum cleaner | To clean dirt and dust | 1901 | |
| Washing machine | To wash clothes | 1908 | |

As you go through the lesson about the colonies, think about how the colonists' lives would have been very different without these and other modern conveniences.

# READ

## The Thirteen Original Colonies

So where exactly were the Thirteen Colonies? Look at the map of the United States. How many states are shown? These states started out as the thirteen original colonies. A **colony** is a place in a different country where a group of people move to start new lives while staying connected to their home country. This is where Europeans from England first started new lives in the New World. The colonies were on the east coast. A **coast** is where land touches a large body of water, like an ocean. Trace your finger along the east coast of the map.

### REGIONS OF THE THIRTEEN COLONIES

The Thirteen Colonies had three different regions. A **region** is an area of land with unique characteristics. The Thirteen Colonies were split up into three different regions: the New England colonies, the Middle colonies, and the Southern colonies. Europeans chose to live in a region based on their motivation for moving to the New World and on the lifestyle they wanted to live.

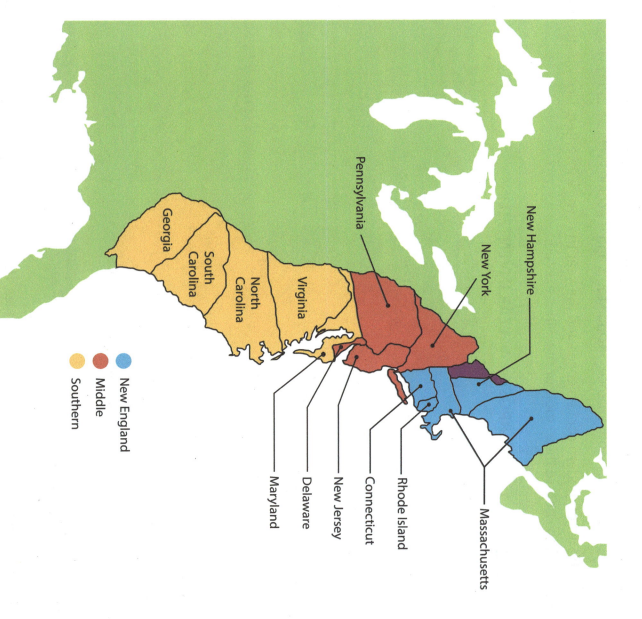

New Hampshire

Pennsylvania

New York

Georgia

South Carolina

North Carolina

Virginia

Maryland

Delaware

New Jersey

Connecticut

Rhode Island

Massachusetts

New England

Middle

Southern

# READ

## Founders of the Colonies

As you have learned, **colonists**—or people who settle in a colony—came to the New World for many reasons. Sometimes colonists moved from one colony to another too. One man named Roger Williams came to the New World to live in Massachusetts Bay. When he began disagreeing with the Puritans' strict laws and punishments, he was forced to leave. He left and **founded** the colony Rhode Island in 1636. This means he started the settlement. Read the table below to learn about more important people in the Thirteen Colonies. Refer back to the map on the last page to find the colonies they founded.

| | |
|---|---|
| **Thomas Hooker** also left Massachusetts Bay because he was unhappy with the Puritans' laws. He founded Connecticut near present-day Hartford. | **William Penn** received money from the King of England to start the colony of Pennsylvania, also known as Penn's Woods. |
| Also known as George Calvert, **Lord Baltimore** was given land in the New World to start the colony of Maryland. | **James Oglethorpe** founded Georgia as a safe place for poor English people. He hoped they would be able to own property and work for themselves. |

English people moved to one of the three regions of the colonies for specific reasons. The New England colonies offered religious freedom. The Middle colonies were known to be the most welcoming as well as were great for farmers, bankers, and businesspeople. The Southern colonies had large farms for growing crops that made a lot of money.

## ONLINE CONNECTION

The Thirteen Colonies have changed a lot since the 1700s! Use a computer to explore the eastern coast of the United States. What big cities exist now? List them below.

........................................

........................................

........................................

........................................

## WRITE

Which region of the Thirteen Colonies would you have wanted to live?

........................................

........................................

........................................

........................................

# READ

## Common Colonial Jobs

When the Pilgrims settled in North America, they did not have a system of money. They traded goods for what they needed, and they spent their time taking care of their land so they could live off of it. As colonists learned how to set up communities more quickly and easily, they began to work away from their homes.

In the 1600s and 1700s, colonists did not have the machines and technology we have today. They had to make everything by hand. In the New England colonies where there were many forests, some colonists became expert shipbuilders and fishermen. In the Southern colonies, crops that farmers could sell for a lot of money were known as **cash crops**. These included tobacco, rice, and cotton. In the Middle colonies, farmers grew wheat and grains to make bread. Banks became popular, and people started their own businesses.

No matter where people lived, there were common jobs people had in the colonies:

- Blacksmiths: used steel and iron to make farm equipment and horseshoes
- Cobblers: made and fixed shoes
- Coopers: made barrels out of wood
- Silversmiths: made dishes and silverware out of silver
- Millers: made grains and corn into flour
- Tailors: made clothing
- Printers: printed newspapers, signs, and books
- Wheelwrights: made and fixed wagons and their wheels

**Which of the jobs listed would have used the shops pictured here?**

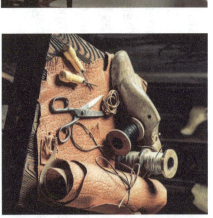

# READ

## Life in Colonial Times

Even though many colonists had begun to work outside of their homes by the 1700s, life was very different from the way we live today. Although people could find blacksmiths, tailors, or cobblers in colonial towns, everything was made by hand. There were no machines to make clothing or print newspapers. Women did many chores around the house. They did laundry by hand, took care of the children, and churned butter. Shops were beginning to sell food, but most colonists made what they could at home.

# PRACTICE

Use the chart below to compare colonial life with the way your family lives today. Write the similarities in the "Both" section. Write the differences in the other two sections.

| COLONIAL LIFE | BOTH | LIFE TODAY |
|---|---|---|
|  |  |  |

## REVIEW

In this lesson, you learned:

- There were different locations for the New England colonies, Middle colonies, and Southern colonies.

- The original colonies were on the east coast of the United States.

- Several important people started different colonies.

- Common colonial jobs in the colonies included coopers, blacksmiths, and tailors.

**Think About It**
What colonial job would you have been interested in if you lived in the colonies?

# SHOW WHAT YOU KNOW

1. Determine in which region each colony was located. Write NE for New England colonies, M for Middle colonies, or S for Southern colonies next to each colony.

Virginia _____        Connecticut _____        South Carolina _____

New Hampshire _____    Rhode Island _____       New Jersey _____

Massachusetts _____    Delaware _____           Pennsylvania _____

Maryland _____         North Carolina _____     Georgia _____

                                                                      New York _____

2. Look at the map to the right. Write which region is shown by each color: New England colonies, Middle colonies, and Southern colonies.

Blue: _____

Red: _____

Yellow: _____

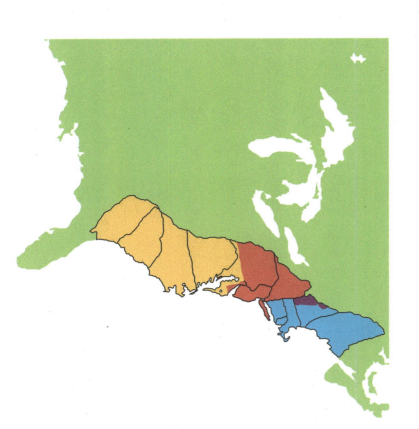

# SHOW WHAT YOU KNOW

Fill in the blanks with the correct words to complete the sentences.

3. The original Thirteen Colonies were located on the _____ coast of the United States.

4. James Oglethorpe started the colony of _____.

5. Sometimes called Penn's Woods, _____ was founded by William Penn.

Read each sentence. Circle True or False.

6. True or False  A blacksmith made farm equipment and horseshoes from iron.

7. True or False  A cobbler made baked goods with flour.

8. True or False  A tailor published books and newspapers.

9. True or False  A cooper made large barrels out of wood.

10. What is one way life today is the same as life in the colonies?

.................................................................................

.................................................................................

11. What is one way life today is different from life in the colonies?

.................................................................................

.................................................................................

# CREATE

As you learned in the lesson, there were many colonial jobs. Create a help wanted poster for a colonial job that could have been hung in one region of the Thirteen Colonies. On the poster, include:

• A picture of something related to the job
• What the person would have to do at the job
• Skills they would need to be successful at the job

# Lesson 8

# Physical Geography

**By the end of this lesson, you will be able to:**

- identify important waterways in the colonies
- describe how colonists used different waterways and their importance

## Lesson Review

If you need to review trade, please go to the lesson titled "Two Worlds Meet."

## Academic Vocabulary

Read the following vocabulary words and definitions. Look through the lesson. Can you find each vocabulary word? Underline the vocabulary word in your lesson. Write the page number of where you found each word in the blanks.

- **tributary:** a smaller river or stream that branches off of a larger river (page ___)
- **waterway:** a body of water people use to travel (page ___)

**IN THE REAL WORLD**

Did you know that about 70 percent of Earth is covered in saltwater? Saltwater is found in oceans and seas. About three percent of water on Earth is fresh water, which is found in lakes and rivers.

On the lines below, write down two or three names of specific bodies of water that fit under each category.

**Salt Water**

........................................

........................................

........................................

**Fresh Water**

........................................

........................................

........................................

# EXPLORE

Have you ever been on a boat? How about fishing? In many places in the United States, you will find a stream, river, bay, or ocean somewhere nearby. People can do a lot of different things with these bodies of water. They can fish or ride on boats. They can swim or water-ski.

Think of things people can do in a body of water like a river or ocean and why they might visit it. Make a list of your ideas below.

........................................................................

........................................................................

........................................................................

People in the colonies also used bodies of water. Do you think they used them for the same reasons you listed, or were their reasons different?

**Atlantic Ocean**

**Hudson River**

# READ

## Waterways in the Colonies

Today, when you need to get from place to place, you probably hop in a vehicle and ride to your destination. What did early Americans do before cars and buses existed?

Many of the colonies were built near or on a river. A river is a type of **waterway**, or a body of water people use to travel. These rivers provided explorers and colonists paths that helped them get from place to place. Most of these rivers connect to the Atlantic Ocean. Let's look at these rivers.

The map below of present-day New York shows the St. Lawrence River, the Hudson River, and the Susquehanna River.

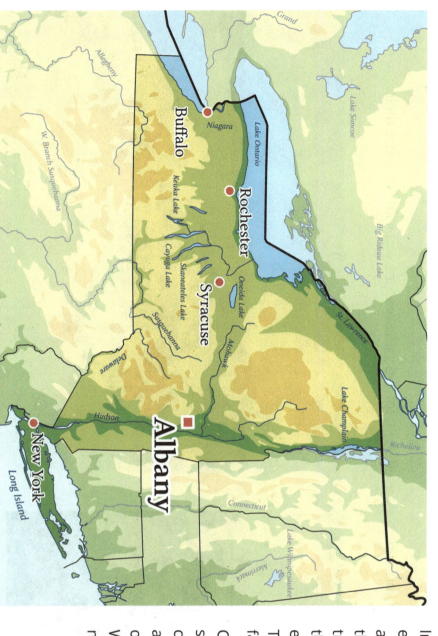

In the colonies, rivers like these were wide enough and deep enough for small ships and boats to travel on. Early explorers used these rivers as routes into the continent. They traveled along the rivers to explore and map the land in the New World. Without rivers, explorers would have had to walk on foot. They probably would not have made it very far inland!

Colonists also used the rivers to trade with settlements nearby. A network of tributaries created a web of waterways to quickly travel across the land. A **tributary** is a smaller river or stream that branches off of a larger river. Without stores to buy materials, trading with nearby communities was important to settlers.

# READ

## More Waterways in the Colonies

If you look at the map of Virginia, you will notice some more important waterways of the colonies. Each number on the map represents one of the following waterways:

**1.** Delaware River

**2.** Potomac River

**3.** Chesapeake Bay

**4.** James River (This is where the colony of Jamestown was located.)

Many early communities were set up near rivers because the fresh water made it easier for settlers to live off of the land. They cleaned and drank the water. They bathed and washed clothes in it. They fished and hunted animals who came to drink out of nearby rivers.

Land around major rivers was usually moist and great for planting crops. In the Middle Colonies, major rivers like the Delaware River provided fertile soil for growing wheat, corn, and orchard fruits. Rivers in the south, like the James River, made the soil fertile for crops like tobacco, rice, and cotton that grew better in warmer climates.

The Chesapeake Bay also provided an easy way to send tobacco and other products back to England. Ships could dock at the mouths of rivers, and people could load or unload goods that would travel back and forth across the Atlantic Ocean.

# WRITE

Why were major rivers and waterways important to early settlers in the colonies?

...............................................................................................

...............................................................................................

# PRACTICE

Draw a picture below to show one way colonists used waterways in the colonies.

## REVIEW

In this lesson, you learned:

- Several rivers made paths from the Atlantic Ocean into the colonies.

- These waterways were important to early settlers' way of life because they provided fresh water for everyday needs. They also provided a way to get from place to place to trade goods.

### Think About It

How do the ways in which early settlers used waterways compare to the ways people use them today?

# SHOW WHAT YOU KNOW

Circle the correct answers for each question.

1. Which major river flows through Virginia?

A. Hudson River

B. Connecticut River

C. James River

D. St. Lawrence River

2. Which major river runs through New York?

A. Potomac River

B. Hudson River

C. Chesapeake River

D. James River

3. Which river is not one of the main waterways colonists used?

A. Colorado River

B. Potomac River

C. Delaware River

D. James River

Read each sentence. Circle True or False.

4. True or False  Colonists used fresh water from rivers for everyday needs such as drinking, bathing, and washing clothes.

5. True or False  Rivers were used as pathways to get from one place to another.

6. True or False  Colonists used rivers mostly for entertainment. They enjoyed spending time on sandy beaches and kayaking.

7. True or False  Colonists fished in rivers and hunted animals that came to drink.

## CREATE

Create your own map of the important waterways in the colonies. This could be a map that you draw, or it could be a three-dimensional map made with clay. You could mold the clay into the shapes of the various rivers and place them on a piece of cardboard. When the clay dries, you could then paint and label the rivers and the rest of your map.

8. True or False  Waterways were an important mode of transportation. Without them, colonists had to walk to get from place to place.

9. True or False  Early explorers did not use rivers at all and only traveled on foot across the land.

10. True or False  Land around rivers provided moist, fertile soil for growing crops.

Discover! SOCIAL STUDIES • GRADE 4 • LESSON 8

61

# Lesson 9

# Cash Crops and Trade

## By the end of this lesson, you will be able to:

- state the meaning of the words *imports* and *exports*
- identify cash crops (tobacco, rice, and indigo) that the Southern Colonies exported and where they were grown
- describe why cash crops were important to Southern Colonies like Virginia and the Carolinas
- describe the reasons for the rise of slavery in the colonies
- describe why Charles Town was important to the Southern Colonies' economy

## Lesson Review

If you need to review what led to the growing of cash crops in the Southern Colonies, please go to the lesson titled "Jamestown."

## Academic Vocabulary

Read the following vocabulary words and definitions. Look through the lesson. Can you find each vocabulary word? Underline the vocabulary word in your lesson. Write the page number of where you found each word in the blanks.

- **cash crops:** crops that grow well in an area and are worth a lot of money when sold (page ___)
- **export:** goods made in a country and shipped out to other places (page ___)
- **import:** goods made and brought into a country from another place (page ___)
- **indigo:** a tropical plant that produces blue dye (page ___)
- **plantation:** a large farm (page ___)
- **port:** a place where ships can load and unload goods (page ___)

# CREATE

Do you remember learning about the Columbian Exchange? This was the system of trade between the New World and Europe. Some of the goods, like food and animals that were common in the New World, were taken to Europe and other goods common in Europe were brought to the New World.

Create a poster to show the movement of goods from Europe and the New World using your knowledge of the Columbian Exchange. Add additional goods to the poster as you learn about them in this lesson.

- **Triangle Trade:** a system of trade between Africa, Europe, and the New World (page ___)
- **slaves:** people who are forced to work without being paid and are seen as property (page ___)

# EXPLORE

Everything in your work space was made somewhere. Where do you think your supplies were made? Where did other products in your home come from?

Some items in your home were probably made in the United States. Others may have been shipped from other countries. Most items have a tag or label that tells where they were made. For example, a cup or dish might say "Made in China" on the bottom, or a pillow on the couch might have a tag that says "Made in Indonesia."

Go on a scavenger hunt around your home and find out where items in your home were made. Keep a tally below. If you find items made in countries other than the US or China, write the country on one of the lines in the left column.

| ORIGINAL COUNTRY | TALLY |
|---|---|
| Made in the *United States* | |
| Made in *China* | |
| Made in | |
| Made in | |
| Made in | |

What conclusions can you draw from your findings? Write at least three observations on the lines. Use the sentence starters to help you.

Most items in my home were made in ........................................................................................

....................................................................................................................................................

I noticed that ...........................................................................................................................

....................................................................................................................................................

Another observation that I made was .............................................................................

....................................................................................................................................................

# READ

## Cash Crops in the South

In previous lessons, you learned what made the New England, Middle, and Southern colonial regions unique. In the Southern Colonies, many people grew and traded cash crops. **Cash crops** are plants that grow well in certain areas and can be sold for a lot of money. Cash crops in the Southern Colonies, like Virginia and the Carolinas, included tobacco, rice, cotton, and indigo. **Indigo** is a tropical plant that produces blue dye. This blue dye is highly valued for coloring fabrics. The warm, damp climate in the Southern Colonies made growing these cash crops easy. The economy of the Southern Colonies depended on the sale of these cash crops, which made these crops very important to them.

Colonists in the South cleared land for large farms, which were called **plantations**, so they could grow as many plants as possible and make as much money as possible. There was only one problem: they could not keep up with all of the work of harvesting their crops on their own.

At first, many plantation owners had indentured servants working on their farms. Indentured servants were workers who did not have the money to travel to the New World. Plantation owners would pay their passage and give them food and shelter in exchange for working on their plantation for about five years. Then the indentured servants earned their freedom. This changed with the rise of slavery in the colonies.

Indigo Plants

Cotton Fields on a Southern Plantation

## The Rise of Slavery

Slavery has existed throughout history and in countries all over the world. When a country set up colonies in a different country, slaves were often used in order to make the colonies as profitable as possible. During the 1600s in Africa, many tribes and communities of Indigenous Africans traded with each other and with countries in Europe. In addition to trading various goods and products, African men, women, and children were also traded to Europeans in the New World. These people were known as **slaves**. These slaves became the property of plantation owners and had to work for them for free.

Many plantation owners in Virginia and the Carolinas began using slaves to plant and harvest more crops. These crops were then sold to other countries for a lot of money. A system of trade developed between Africa, Europe, and the New World. This system became known as the **Triangle Trade**, and it existed for almost 200 years.

Look at the map to the right. Trace your finger along the trade routes. What do you notice? What kind of shape do the trade routes make?

### TRADING INCREASES

In the 1600s and 1700s, colonists in the New World traded cash crops and other goods around the world. In the colonies, large amounts of cash crops from the Southern Colonies were exported to Europe. **Exports** are goods made in a country and taken to other places around the world to be sold or traded. In Europe, where technology was more advanced, these goods were made into products in factories and then sold or traded. Goods such as clothing and processed foods were taken to Africa and traded for slaves. Slaves were then **imported**, or brought into, North America from Africa to work on plantations and produce more crops.

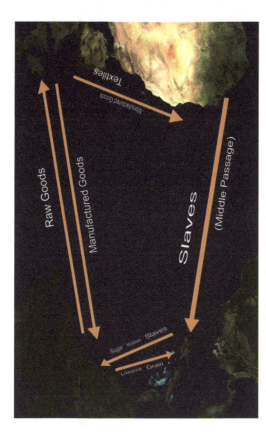

*Detailed Triangle Trade.jpg by Supportstorm, including images sourced from NASA, is in the public domain.*

**WRITE**

Explain the Triangle Trade system. Include the meaning of the words *imports* and *exports*.

........................................................

........................................................

........................................................

........................................................

........................................................

........................................................

# READ

## Charles Town Port

Waterways, like rivers, were important to the colonies for many reasons. They helped colonists survive and travel, but they also helped the early economy in the colonies. Today, you might go to a store and exchange money for an item you want. This is an example of how today's economy works. In colonial times, before people bought goods with money, they traded what they had for what they wanted.

In the New England colonies, there were many rivers full of freshwater fish. Settlers there became expert fishermen and were able to trade fish.

Charles Town, in South Carolina, was important to the Southern Colonies' economy and to the Triangle Trade system because of its port. A **port** is a place where ships can load and unload goods. The port in Charles Town was close to many southern plantations, so it was convenient for exporting cash crops and for importing slaves from Africa to work on the large farms.

In this modern-day picture, a cargo ship carries supplies into a port.

# REVIEW

In this lesson, you learned:

- Imports and exports refer to goods brought into, and taken out of, a country.

- Cash crops, such as tobacco, rice, and indigo, were grown and exported from the Southern Colonies.

- Cash crops built and strengthened the economy in the Southern Colonies.

- Plantations led to the rise of slavery in the colonies.

- Charles Town was an important port that imported and exported goods for the Southern Colonies.

## Think About It

How do you think the Southern Colonies would be different if slaves had not worked on plantations?

# PRACTICE

Create a map to illustrate the Triangle Trade by following these directions.

1. On the map, label the three continents involved in the Triangle Trade system: North America, Europe, and Africa.

2. Where the lines meet near the New World, write *Charles Town.*

3. Draw arrows to indicate which ways trade moved between continents, and label each line with the exports that were shipped from one place to another.

Today, Americans have the right to life, liberty, and the pursuit of happiness, but this was not always true. Slaves were considered property. Their owners controlled their lives. Enslaved people were treated very poorly and denied many rights on southern plantations.

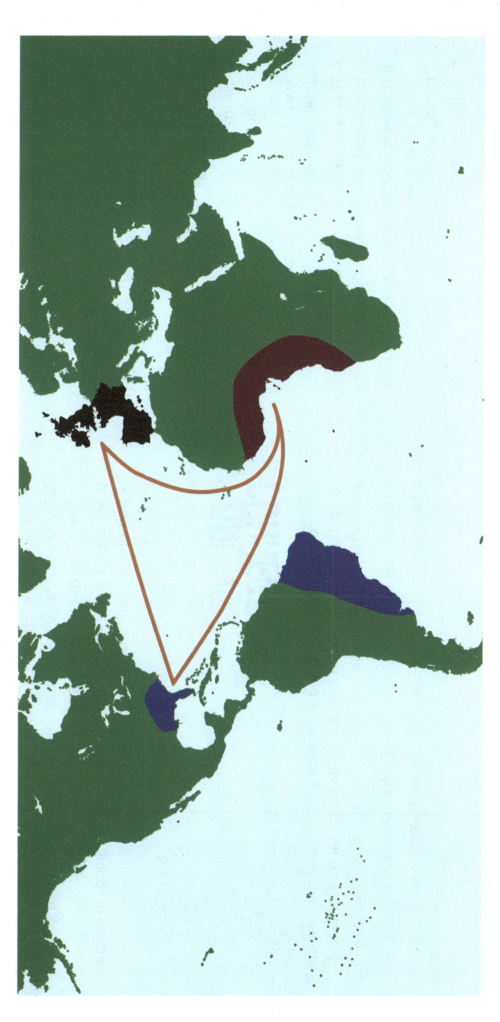

# WHAT SHOW YOU KNOW

Circle the correct answer to each question.

1. An _____ is a good made and brought into a country from another place.

   A. import

   B. export

   C. indigo

2. An _____ is a good made in a country and shipped out to other places.

   A. import

   B. export

   C. Triangle Trade

3. What cash crops were exported from Southern Colonies like Virginia and the Carolinas?

   A. orchard fruits, wheat, and oats

   B. fish, trees, and beavers

   C. tobacco, rice, indigo, and cotton

4. Why were cash crops important to the Southern Colonies?

   A. They were exported and traded for other goods that helped the colonies' early economy.

   B. They were worth a lot of money, so the New World became an important part of a worldwide trading system.

   C. Both A and B

5. What led to the rise in slavery in the New World?

   A. Europeans in the Southern Colonies bought or traded slave workers for their plantations so they could produce more cash crops.

   B. Europeans in the Southern Colonies thought slaves had gold, so they brought them to the New World to steal from them.

   C. Slaves encouraged others from Africa to join them in the New World.

6. Why was Charles Town important to the Southern Colonies' economy?

   A. There was a large port on the water where ships imported goods and slaves and where cash crops were exported to Europe.

   B. Southern Colonies did not have to transport their goods to another part of the colonies before exporting them.

   C. Both A and B

## ONLINE CONNECTION

Use a computer to research and then create a digital presentation about one of the following African Americans who fought for the freedom of slaves in the United States.

- Harriet Tubman
- Sojourner Truth
- Fredrick Douglass
- Anna J. Cooper

# Lesson 10

## Chapter 1 Review

### By the end of this lesson, you will:

- review the information from the lessons in Chapter 1, "The New World."

### Lesson Review

Throughout the chapter, we have learned the following big ideas:

- Columbus landed in North America while searching for a new trade route. (Lesson 1)

- Jamestown was the first permanent English settlement in the New World. (Lesson 2)

- The Pilgrims and Puritans both came to settle in the New World, but they were different in many ways. (Lessons 3 and 6)

- The Mayflower Compact was a document that outlined how Plymouth Colony would be governed, and it still influences American government today. (Lesson 4)

- Indigenous people were impacted by the arrival of settlers in the New World. (Lesson 5)

- The colonies were divided into three regions that each had unique characteristics: New England Colonies, Middle Colonies, and Southern Colonies. (Lesson 7)

- There were many waterways in the colonies that were important to the colonists for survival and transportation. (Lesson 8)

- Cash crops were important to the Southern Colonies and an important part of the Triangle Trade with Europe and Africa. (Lesson 9)

Go back and review the lessons as needed while you complete the activities.

## PLAY

Using what you have learned about the New World and the establishment of the first colonies, pretend you are a colonist or an Indigenous person. Role play what a "day in your life" might have looked like. For example, act out a job colonists may have had or how an Indigenous person may have farmed or hunted.

# REVIEW

## The New World

In this chapter, we learned that the story of America begins with the accidental "discovery" of the New World. In 1492, Christopher Columbus left Europe in search of a new trade route to Asia. He thought his ship landed in Asia, but he was actually in the Caribbean Islands in North America. He called this the New World. However, Columbus was not the first person to discover this place, as he found Indigenous people who were already living there.

Over time, European countries began to send people over to explore and start colonies. Countries wanted more land, and people wanted to start new lives. Some people wanted to get rich, while others wanted the freedom to practice their religion.

In 1607, Jamestown became the first permanent English settlement in North America. Settlers in Jamestown suffered through a long winter before their settlement was successful—not with gold, as they had originally thought, but by selling tobacco.

Other groups like the Pilgrims and Puritans came to the New World as well. The Pilgrims were motivated by religious freedom to settle in North America. The first winter was hard for the Pilgrims because they were not prepared for the cold. Indigenous people from the Wampanoag tribe helped the Pilgrims survive by teaching them how to harvest crops and by trading with them. The Puritans also left England and went to the New World for religious freedom, but they wanted to purify the Church of England's teachings instead of leaving it altogether like the Pilgrims. They founded Massachusetts Bay, where they worked hard, practiced their religion, and followed strict laws.

17th-Century English Village in Plimoth Patuxet Museums

## The Mayflower Compact

One lasting influence from the first colonies is the Mayflower Compact. This was an agreement that detailed how the government would work in Plymouth Colony. It was important because it set up a government that was run by the colonists themselves. The democracy described in this document has influenced American government for hundreds of years.

## Indigenous People and Colonists

As the colonists began to set up permanent residences and governments, the lives of the Indigenous people of North America were greatly impacted. The cultures of the colonists and Indigenous people often clashed. Indigenous people were upset when colonists tried to settle on their tribal lands. This was mainly because Indigenous people did not view land as something that could be owned, while the colonists did. Regardless, colonists and Indigenous people often bartered with each other during times of peace.

**Wampanoag Home**

## The Thirteen Colonies

Over time, the colonies grew to thirteen colonies located along the east coast. The colonies could be divided up into three geographic regions: New England, Middle Colonies, and Southern Colonies. Each region had its own characteristics. For example, the Southern Colonies grew cash crops like tobacco, indigo, and cotton, which led to the rise of plantations and eventually slavery. This also led to the Triangle Trade of imports and exports between North America, Europe, and Africa.

Colonists traveled between areas using different waterways like rivers and the Chesapeake Bay. No matter where colonists would travel, they would often find people working similar types of jobs. Even though the colonies were spread across the east coast, the people in them all worked hard to make a new life in the New World.

# PRACTICE

## Visualizing Vocabulary

Draw a picture of each vocabulary word to help you remember its meaning.

COLONY

MAYFLOWER COMPACT

BARTER

COLUMBIAN EXCHANGE

IMPORT

EXPORT

# PRACTICE

## New World Timeline

On the timeline below, write the letters from the following events in the blanks to show the order in which they occurred.

**A.** Columbus writes about his journeys, motivating more people to come to the New World.

**B.** Jamestown becomes the first permanent English settlement in North America.

**C.** New colonies are founded, and eventually thirteen colonies line the east coast.

**D.** Columbus lands in the New World while looking for a trade route to Asia.

**E.** The Puritans and Pilgrims settle in the New World.

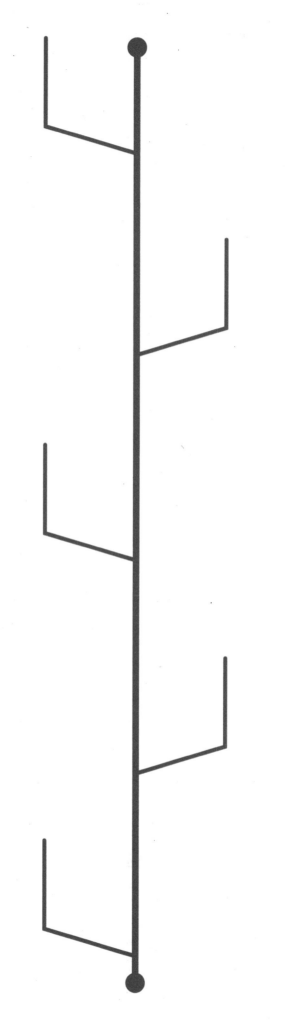

# PRACTICE

## Causes and Effects

Fill in the organizer below with causes and effects from the chapter. Think about events that happened in the early part of American history and why they happened. The "cause" is why it happened, and the "effect" is what happened as a result. An example has been done for you.

| CAUSE | EFFECT |
|---|---|
| Columbus was looking for a new trade route to Asia. | He landed in North America and thought he "discovered" the New World. |
| Cash crops like cotton and tobacco made the Southern Colonies a lot of money. | |
| The Puritans had very strict laws. | |
| | Many colonists traveled on waterways to quickly get to faraway places to trade. |

## SHOW WHAT YOU KNOW

Think about what you've learned about in this chapter. Circle how you feel:

4 – I know this chapter really well. I could teach it to someone.

3 – I know this chapter pretty well.

2 – I am still learning this chapter. I am not sure about some things.

1 – I am confused. I have a lot of questions about what I've learned.

Talk to your instructor about your answers. When you're ready, ask your instructor for the Show What You Know activity for the chapter.

# WRITE

Think about your learning. What stands out to you in the lessons? What questions do you have? What do you wonder about? You can use this page to take notes, write out your responses, and then discuss them with your instructor.

# Chapter 2
## A New Country

Good day! Monty the Lion reporting for action!

Last time we chatted, I was on my way to Boston with my wife Maria and best buddy Leo. Our journey to America was quite the adventure.

Typically, I would fly over to America. However, my buddy Leo is afraid of heights. That's the honest truth, I'm not lyin'!

So, we decided to catch a ride on a ship across the Atlantic Ocean instead. That's when our journey really starts to get rocky.

I remember learning about similar voyages that took place in American History. Did you know that the Pilgrims left England in search of religious freedom and a fresh start in the New World?

They boarded a large ship like the one Maria, Leo, and I took. Their ship was named the Mayflower. I really like that name! It reminds me of warm hugs. Our ship on the other hand was named the Sea Urchin, and its name certainly matched the personality of the crew members. Very prickly people to say the least.

We all had to be very brave for our trip across the ocean. I did not realize it at the moment, but this was the start of my inner leadership skills getting ready to roar!

# What Will I Learn?

This chapter examines the road to the Revolutionary War. It dives into the events that helped shape the view of colonists toward Great Britain and their want for an independent United States of America.

## Lessons at a Glance

# Lesson 11

# French and Indian War

## By the end of this lesson, you will be able to:

- identify the causes of the French and Indian War
- describe why the British wanted to gain land during the French and Indian War

## Lesson Review

If you need to review relationships between colonists and Indigenous people, please go to the lesson titled "Two Worlds Meet."

## Academic Vocabulary

Read the following vocabulary words and definitions. Look through the lesson. Can you find each vocabulary word? Underline the vocabulary word in your lesson. Write the page number of where you found each word in the blanks.

- **allies:** two groups who agree to help each other (page ___)
- **basin:** a large bowl-shaped dip in the land (page ___)
- **rivals:** people or groups of people who compete with each other for the same thing (page ___)

### IN THE REAL WORLD

Think about a time when you had to choose between two things. Maybe you had to choose between having ice cream or cake for dessert. Perhaps you were able to choose your own birthday gift and had to decide between two toys that you really wanted. How were you able to decide which thing you wanted more? What made choosing between two things difficult or easy?

It can be easier to choose between two good things, like dessert or toys. What if you had to choose between doing the dishes or cleaning your room? You might not want to do either of those things, so how would you decide? Think about which chore you would choose and why you would choose it. Discuss your ideas with your instructor.

# EXPLORE

Have you ever had a hard time agreeing on something with a sibling or a friend because you both wanted different things? Maybe you couldn't decide which movie to watch, and you only had time to watch one. Maybe you had to agree on which game to play, but each of you wanted to play something different. What happened when you couldn't agree? Did the two of you get upset? Did you start arguing?

Disputes like this can happen between two people, but they can also happen between two countries. What kinds of things might two countries disagree about? What might happen if they cannot come to an agreement that both countries are happy with? Write your ideas on the lines below.

# PLAY

Look at the image below. The two children are competing against each other in a game of tennis. Ask a sibling or your instructor to play a game with you. As you play, pay attention to how you feel during the competition. Do you compete intensely to win?

People can compete against each other in games, but countries can also compete against each other. They might compete for land or resources. This competition can then lead to conflict like the French and Indian War.

# READ

## The Ohio River Basin

In the 1750s, most of the land in North America was claimed by France and England, also known as Great Britain. During this time, the two countries were rivals. **Rivals** are people or groups of people who compete with each other for the same thing. Fighting between Great Britain and France was common in the 1700s. One disagreement, in particular, between the two countries caused the French and Indian War.

Look at the map below. Point to the area labeled "Ohio River Basin." A **basin** is a large bowl-shaped dip in the land. In the 1750s, Great Britain had control of the land in the colonies. Write "British" on the map over the land to the right of the Ohio River Basin, where the colonies existed.

France had claimed the land in the Ohio River Basin. Write "French" on the map over the Ohio River Basin in a different color.

France had used the land in the Ohio River Basin for a long time to trade with Indigenous peoples for animal fur. In France, animal fur was very fashionable, making it very valuable. France had a good fur trading business in the area with Indigenous peoples who wanted guns and ammunition from Europe. Great Britain was also interested in the resources of the Ohio River Basin. They wanted the land so badly, they were willing to go to war with France to get it. This land was the cause of the French and Indian War.

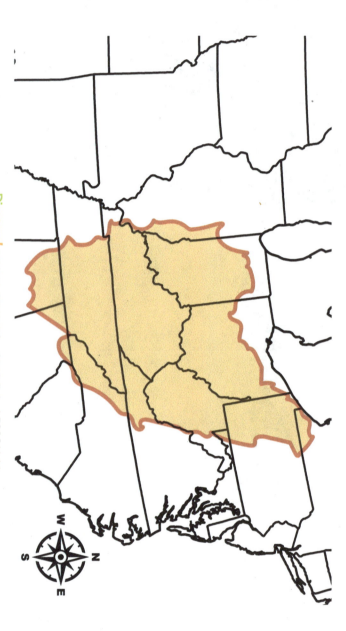

# READ

## Great Britain's Desire for More

Great Britain wanted the land in the Ohio River Basin for two main reasons. First, the population in the colonies was growing. Great Britain wanted to gain the land in the Ohio River Basin to expand the colonies. Second, Great Britain also thought the land was an excellent economic opportunity. Colonists knew the soil around the Ohio River was great for farming, and they knew gaining control of the land would increase their ability to trade.

## INDIGENOUS PEOPLES IN THE AREA

Many tribes of Indigenous peoples were also interested in the land in the Ohio River Basin. They had lived on the land for a long time and had benefited from trading with the French. They did not want Great Britain to take over, so they sided with the French. Other tribes sided with Great Britain.

There were other reasons that certain tribes chose to support the French or the British. Some of the different tribes of Indigenous peoples did not get along before the French and Indian War began. They were rivals with one another, just like France and England. Because of this, if one tribe sided with the French, a rival tribe would side with the British and become their allies. **Allies** are two groups who agree to help each other in certain situations, such as wars.

Other Indigenous tribes did not want to fight in the war at all. They simply wished to keep their land. However, they were less powerful than the Europeans, who had access to guns and cannons. Ultimately, they were forced to choose sides.

## ONLINE CONNECTION

You might not know that George Washington not only began his military career during the French and Indian War but he might have helped start it! Colonel Washington led his men into battle against the French at Jumonville Glen, which is considered to be the first battle of the war. With your instructor, go online to find more information about Washington's role in the French and Indian War.

# PRACTICE

Think about what you have learned about the French and Indian War in this lesson. Read the causes below and match each to its effect.

## CAUSES

1. _____ The land in the Ohio River Basin was controlled by the French, but it was close to the British colonies.

2. _____ The French had been using the land for years to trade with local Indigenous people.

3. _____ The British wanted the land near the Ohio River to expand their colonies and because it would be good for farming.

4. _____ Many tribes of Indigenous peoples did not want to join either side, but they were not able to fight for their land on their own.

5. _____ Some Indigenous tribes were rivals with the tribes that sided with France.

## EFFECTS

A. The French wanted to keep the land and continue their trading business with the local tribes of Indigenous peoples.

B. Some Indigenous tribes became allies with the British because their rivals were allies with the French.

C. Some tribes of Indigenous peoples were forced to pick sides in the French and Indian War.

D. Both the French and the British wanted the land.

E. British colonists were willing to go to war with the French to gain control of the land, expand their colonies, and use the land for farming.

# REVIEW

In this lesson, you learned:

- The rivalry between the British and French over the Ohio River Basin caused the French and Indian War.

- The British wanted the Ohio River Basin for its fertile land, access to the fur trade, and so that more colonists could settle in the west.

- The French wanted the land to continue their fur trade with the Indigenous tribes.

- Some tribes of Indigenous peoples chose to take sides in the war, but others were forced to take sides to save their land.

## Think About It

The French and the British both wanted the land in the Ohio River Basin so much that they were willing to go to war for it. What else might they have done to reach an agreement?

## SHOW WHAT YOU KNOW

Fill in the blanks with the correct words to complete the sentences.

1. The major cause of the French and Indian War was the desire for land in the _____ River Basin.

2. The French wanted the land because they wanted to expand their trading business with the _____ people.

3. The British wanted the land because it had great soil for _____.

4. The British also wanted the land to _____ their colonies.

5. Indigenous tribes who were rivals with those who sided with the French became _____ to the British.

6. The French and Indian War was a war in which the French and many Indigenous tribes fought against the _____.

7. Explain the major causes of the French and Indian War.

   _____
   _____
   _____
   _____
   _____

## ONLINE CONNECTION

The popularity of beaver felt hats in Europe helped the fur trade because beaver pelts became very valuable. The Indigenous peoples harvested the pelts and sold them to fur trading companies in North America, which sold them to different manufacturers all across Europe. The pelts were made into hats, capes, and other articles of clothing.

Other animal furs were also popular and in demand. With your instructor, go online to find out which types of furs were used in the fashion industry and how the demand for furs benefited the Indigenous peoples, the traders, and others.

Beaver Pelt

# Lesson 12

# Results of the French and Indian War

**By the end of this lesson, you will be able to:**

- describe how the French and Indian War changed life in the colonies
- summarize the differences in which countries controlled parts of North America after the French and Indian War

## Lesson Review

If you need to review the French and Indian War, please go to the lesson titled "French and Indian War."

## Academic Vocabulary

Read the following vocabulary word and definition. Look through the lesson. Can you find the vocabulary word? Underline the vocabulary word in your lesson. Write the page number of where you found the word in the blank.

- **Treaty of Paris (1763):** an agreement between the French and British to stop fighting (page ___)

## PLAY

The British, French, and Indigenous people all fought in the French and Indian War for control of the land in the Ohio River Basin. The British wanted to expand the colonies and use the land for farming. The French wanted to continue their fur trading business with the Indigenous people, who took sides to keep their land.

Choose a group of people involved in the war. Pretend you are a leader in the group, and explain to your people why you think it is important to fight for the land in the Ohio River Basin.

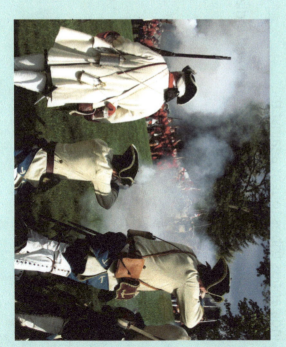

# EXPLORE

Where do great leaders come from? What helps them learn how to be great leaders? It can take a long time to learn how to become a great leader. All great leaders have made mistakes. Often, they learn from these mistakes, and that is what helps them to become great leaders.

You probably know George Washington as the first president of the United States, but did you know that he fought in the French and Indian War before he was a president?

George Washington made a big impact on the colonies and the early United States. When he became president, it was because people voted for him to be their leader! What do you think makes a strong leader? What kinds of qualities does a strong leader have?

## PLAY

Get a few friends and family members together to play a game of Follow the Leader. Take turns being the leader and having the other players follow you while imitating what you do. You might jump up and down, walk in a circle, clap your hands, skip, hop, or do other fun things.

Each new leader should try to do things that the other leaders have not. Try to come up with things that are fun, like dancing, marching, or moving your hands and arms in different ways!

# READ

## A Brief Recap

You have already learned some information about the French and Indian War. In this war, Great Britain and a few tribes of Indigenous people fought against France and several other tribes of Indigenous people over the land in the Ohio River Basin. France wanted the land to keep their fur trading business with the Indigenous people who lived in the area, and Great Britain wanted to expand the colonies and use the land for farming.

## THE END OF THE WAR

Many battles were fought during the French and Indian War between 1754 and 1763. The war finally ended when the **Treaty of Paris (1763)** was signed, which was an agreement between the French and British to stop fighting. The agreement gave control of the land in the Ohio River Basin to Great Britain.

After the war, Great Britain controlled all of the land in the eastern part of North America and Canada. Before the war, they really only controlled the Thirteen Colonies and part of eastern Canada. France had given its land west of the Mississippi River to Spain. After the war ended in 1763, France no longer had any land in North America, except for a few islands south of Florida.

On the map to the right, trace the Mississippi River in blue. Color the land to the west of it yellow and label it "Spain." Color the land to the east of it red and label it "Great Britain."

Mississippi River

# READ

## Effects on the Colonies

In the weeks following the French and Indian War, British colonists felt a sense of relief. They no longer lived in fear of their French rivals nearby. They were also excited about new land and farming opportunities west of the colonies. With new land in Florida, where some crops grew well, plantation owners were able to expand their trade businesses.

Life in the colonies was very different for Indigenous people after the French and Indian War too. Since most of them had fought with France, they were surrounded by enemies on Great Britain's newly gained land. Indigenous people who fought with France were upset about losing the war, and they were afraid the British would force them to leave their homes so that the British could use that land to farm. Indigenous people tried attacking the British many times.

# WRITE

Which countries controlled different parts of North America after the French and Indian War?

.................................................................

.................................................................

.................................................................

.................................................................

.................................................................

# ONLINE CONNECTION

Research online to find out more about the Treaty of Paris. See if you can answer the questions below:

- Where was the Treaty of Paris signed?
- Who signed it?
- How long did the agreement take?
- Besides France giving up their land in North America, were any other agreements made?

**The painting *Treaty of Paris* by Benjamin West remained unfinished due to the incompliance of some treaty members.**

*Treaty of Paris by Benjamin West 1783.jpg by Benjamin West is in the public domain.*

# PRACTICE

Use the boxes to compare North America from before and after the French and Indian War. Include information about which countries controlled specific parts of North America after the war and how different groups of people may have felt before and after the war.

**BEFORE THE WAR**

**AFTER THE WAR**

## REVIEW

In this lesson, you learned:

- The French and Indian War made life better for the British colonists.

- Life for the Indigenous tribes that had sided with France became worse after the war.

- Maps of North America changed significantly after the French and Indian War.

- England gained a lot of land after the war, but France lost a lot of its land.

### Think About It

How might the relationship between the British and Indigenous people change if the British expanded the colonies and used the land in the Ohio River Basin for farming? Do you think that the Indigenous people were willing to move somewhere else so that the British could expand their colonies?

# SHOW WHAT YOU KNOW

Circle the correct answer for each question.

**1.** Before the French and Indian War, _____ controlled land west of the Mississippi River. After the war, _____ controlled the land west of the Mississippi River.

**A.** Great Britain; France

**B.** France; Spain

**C.** Spain; Great Britain

**D.** Indigenous people; France

**2.** Before the French and Indian War, _____ controlled the Ohio River Basin. After the war, _____ controlled the Ohio River Basin.

**A.** Great Britain; Indigenous people

**B.** France; Great Britain

**C.** Spain; Great Britain

**D.** Indigenous people; Spain

**3.** Describe who controlled the land in the Thirteen Colonies before and after the French and Indian War.

**A.** The Thirteen Colonies were controlled by Great Britain before and after the French and Indian War.

**B.** Before the war, Great Britain controlled the colonies; after the war, Spain controlled the colonies.

**C.** Before the war, Great Britain controlled the colonies; after the war, Indigenous people controlled the colonies.

**D.** Before the war, France controlled the colonies; after the war, Great Britain controlled the colonies.

**4.** After the French and Indian War, the British colonists felt _____.

**A.** happy and excited about their new land

**B.** sad and discouraged because many soldiers joined France

**C.** homesick for England

**5.** After the French and Indian War, Indigenous people _____.

**A.** moved to the west coast of North America

**B.** decided to live in British communities and adjust to the British way of living

**C.** feared the British would force them to leave their land, so they tried attacking the British many times

## IN THE REAL WORLD

Can you think of disagreements that countries have with each other today? Talk with your instructor about current events that involve disputes between countries. Discuss why the countries are disagreeing with each other. Write down your findings on the lines below.

...........................................

...........................................

...........................................

...........................................

# Lesson 13

# Tensions

**By the end of this lesson, you will be able to:**

- analyze why there was conflict between the colonies and Britain
- identify events that happened between the French and Indian War and the Boston Massacre

## Lesson Review

If you need to review the French and Indian War, please go to the lessons titled "French and Indian War" and "Results of the French and Indian War."

## Academic Vocabulary

Read the following vocabulary words and definitions. Look through the lesson. Can you find each vocabulary word? Underline the vocabulary word in your lesson. Write the page number of where you found each word in the blanks.

- **acts:** laws (page ___)
- **debt:** money that is owed (page ___)
- **Proclamation Line:** an imaginary line along the Appalachian Mountains that kept colonists and Indigenous people separated to avoid conflict (page ___)
- **tax:** an amount of money collected by the government (page ___)
- **tension:** showing feelings of being worried, nervous, or upset (page ___)

Create a timeline to show the events you have learned about. Include the following:

- 1492 – Columbus found the New World as he searched for a trade route to Asia
- 1607 – Jamestown, in Virginia, was settled
- 1620 – The Pilgrims arrived in Plymouth on the *Mayflower*
- 1630 – The Puritans settled in Massachusetts Bay
- 1754 – The French and Indian War began between France and Great Britain
- 1763 – Great Britain won the French and Indian War

Be on the lookout for more events to add to your timeline throughout this lesson!

# EXPLORE

Have you ever wondered where the money to pay for police and fire departments comes from? What about the money that it costs to make sure that the roads that we drive on every day are safe and secure? The money for those and other public services come from taxes that people and businesses pay. A **tax** is an amount of money collected by the government.

## IN THE REAL WORLD

Some taxes are used to pay for services that keep people safe, like police and fire departments. Did you know that other taxes are used to pay for other things that are beneficial, like libraries and parks?

Work with your instructor to find out what taxes pay for in your community. Make a list of your findings below.

......................................................

......................................................

......................................................

......................................................

......................................................

......................................................

......................................................

......................................................

What might happen if the government did not collect taxes? Write your answers on the lines below.

......................................................

......................................................

......................................................

......................................................

# READ

## Tension Grows in the Colonies

After the French and Indian War when Great Britain took control of the land between the Mississippi River and the Appalachian Mountains, many colonists moved west to build new homes and clear land for farms. This did not make some of the Indigenous people happy. New farms would mean the homes of Indigenous people would be moved. The land they were familiar with would change. Indigenous people did not want to leave their homes.

There were also some French settlers who had not moved after the French and Indian War. These settlers did not want to leave their homes either. Since King George of Great Britain wanted peace, his solution was to forbid the colonists from moving west of the Appalachian Mountains. He made a law called the Proclamation of 1763 by drawing a line along the Appalachian Mountains. This **Proclamation Line** was an imaginary line that kept colonists separated from the remaining French settlers and the Indigenous people. King George ordered colonists to stay east of the line.

The colonists were not happy about the Proclamation Line. They wanted to use land west of the Appalachian Mountains for farming. This law made colonists angry at the king, and tension began to grow. **Tension** means people show feelings of being worried, nervous, or upset. Many colonists were upset because they felt that the British government was being unfair. They also felt that the British government did not have the right to tell them what they could or could not do.

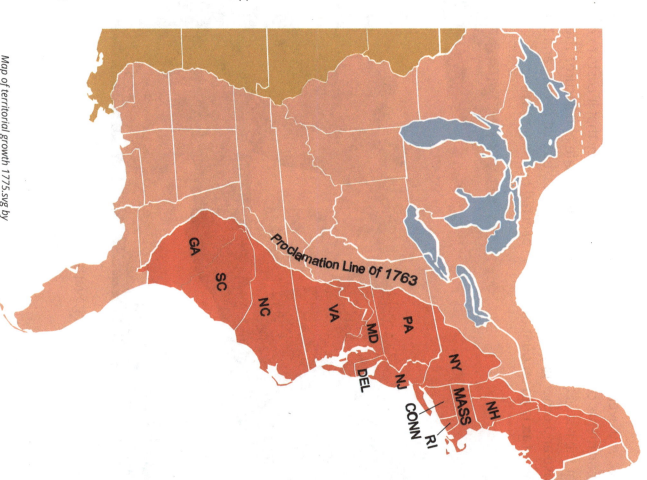

Map of territorial growth 1775.svg by Cg-realms is in the public domain.

# READ

## A Large Debt

One reason that the British government wanted to avoid more conflict was because of the huge debt that they owed from the French and Indian War. A **debt** is an amount of money someone agrees to pay back after borrowing it. The British government had borrowed large sums of money from British and Dutch bankers. They needed this money to pay for the soldiers, forts, and weapons to fight the war. They wanted to avoid more conflict since it would make this debt even bigger.

To pay off this debt, Great Britain decided to tax colonists on goods that they used. They thought it was reasonable to ask the colonists to help pay for the French and Indian War. The colonists, on the other hand, worked hard for their money and did not want to help pay for the war. The taxes created more tension and conflict between the colonies and Great Britain.

## The First Taxes

In 1764, Great Britain began taxing colonists on items by passing various **acts,** or laws. There were many acts that made the tension worse between the colonies and Great Britain. One such act was the Sugar Act in 1764. This required colonists to pay taxes on sugar that was imported from non-British Caribbean sources.

The Sugar Act upset the colonists so much that they boycotted, or stopped buying, certain British luxury goods. Many merchants began making some of these goods themselves. The anger and unrest caused by the Sugar Act led to its being repealed in 1765.

**Colonists were taxed on sugar that was not imported by Britain.**

# READ

## The Stamp Act

Shortly after the Sugar Act was repealed, the Stamp Act was passed in 1765. This placed taxes on all printed materials, including playing cards, newspapers, and magazines. A large stamp on the item indicated that the tax had been paid.

The colonists protested and boycotted British goods once again. The British government repealed it in 1766. However, they also passed the Declaratory Act, which stated that the British government had the right to create laws for the colonies and to tax them.

With each new act, colonists became more and more upset. They believed that these taxes were unfair because they did not have a representative in the British government. If the colonists had a representative in the British government, that person could help decide how much tax was charged and how the money would be used. The colonists grew more unhappy with "taxation without representation."

## The Townshend Acts

In 1767, the British government passed the Townshend Acts. These acts placed indirect taxes, called duties, on imported British goods such as china, glass, paint, lead, paper, and tea. The colonists protested for once again being taxed without proper representation. They also boycotted British goods. The tension between the colonists and the British government became worse and would continue to do so in the years to come.

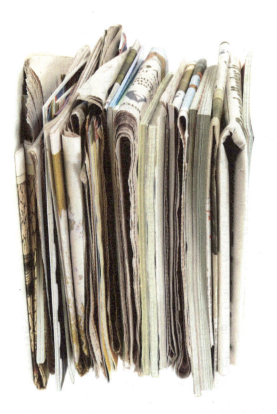

**The Stamp Act taxed colonists on items such as newspapers.**

**The Townshend Acts taxed colonists on items such a tea.**

# PRACTICE

Draw pictures or write words and phrases in the box that describe the reasons for the tension between the colonies and Great Britain.

## REVIEW

In this lesson, you learned:

- The French and Indian War was costly for the British government.

- The British government thought that the colonists should repay the costs of the French and Indian War.

- The Sugar Act, Stamp Act, and Townshend Acts were passed and repealed.

- The colonists thought that taxation without representation was unfair.

On your timeline from page 1, add the following details:

- 1763 – The Proclamation Line separated colonists and Indigenous people

- 1764 – King George began taxing colonists to repay his war debt with the Sugar Act

- 1765 – The Stamp Act taxed newspapers and playing cards

- 1767 – The Townshend Acts taxed paper, paint, and tea

# SHOW WHAT YOU KNOW

1. Sequence the events by ordering them from 1 (first) to 6 (last).

_____ King George passed the Stamp Act, which taxed colonists on all papers in the colonies.

_____ Great Britain fought in the French and Indian War and won the land between the Mississippi River and the Appalachian Mountains.

_____ Conflict between the colonies and Britain grew as the Townshend Act was passed, placing a tax on glass, paint, and tea.

_____ King George passed a law called the Proclamation of 1763 that ordered colonists to stay east of the Appalachian Mountains and Indigenous people to stay west. This angered many colonists.

_____ As colonists moved west of the Appalachian Mountains, many conflicts arose between colonists and Indigenous people.

_____ To pay off his debt from the French and Indian War, King George began taxing colonists on goods they used every day with the Sugar Act.

Read each sentence. Circle True or False.

2. True or False   Tension grew between the colonies and Great Britain because King George drew the Proclamation Line and ordered colonists to stay west of the Appalachian Mountains.

3. True or False   To pay his debts, King George began paying colonists for helping Britain win the war.

4. True or False   Taxes increased tension in the colonies.

5. True or False   The Stamp Act charged a tax on all horses in the colonies.

6. True or False   The Townshend Acts charged a tax on land throughout the colonies.

# ONLINE CONNECTION

With an adult's help, use a search engine to find out more about how the Stamp Act led to the creation of the Sons and Daughters of Liberty. Both groups of colonists felt that taxation without representation was unfair, and both protested in different ways. Compare and contrast their methods of protesting. Discuss your findings with your instructor.

# Lesson 14

## Boston Massacre

### By the end of this lesson, you will be able to:

- compare and contrast the different viewpoints of the Boston Massacre
- compare and contrast colonists' feelings about paying taxes to England
- summarize the different ways colonists reacted to England's laws in the colonies

### Lesson Review

If you need to review reasons for tensions in the colonies, please go to the lesson titled "Tensions."

### Academic Vocabulary

Read the following vocabulary words and definitions. Look through the lesson. Can you find each vocabulary word? Underline the vocabulary word in your lesson. Write the page number of where you found each word in the blanks.

- **boycott:** a protest in which people do not pay for or use a product or service (page ____)
- **Loyalists:** colonists who supported Britain ruling the colonies (page ____)
- **Patriots:** colonists who supported the colonies having independence from Britain (page ____)
- **protest:** to speak out against (page ____)

## IN THE REAL WORLD

### Differing Opinions

Sometimes two people can have different thoughts and opinions about a certain situation or event. They might disagree about whether an idea is good or bad.

Think about a situation or topic in your own community, state, or the country where groups of people have different opinions. For example, your community might have people who disagree on where to build a new dog park. Describe the situation or topic on the lines below. Then think about why each group might think their opinion is correct.

................................................

................................................

................................................

................................................

Take a look at the picture below. What do you see? Do you see a vase? Do you see two people looking at each other? Do you see both?

Look at the image below. Do you see a rabbit or a duck? It all depends on your perspective!

If one person only sees the vase and another person only sees the two people, we might say that they have different perspectives of this picture. That means that they are seeing the same thing in different ways. We can have different perspectives about many things, like ideas or situations. It can be useful to try to see others' perspectives. Doing so can help us to get along better and to avoid things like disagreements and arguments.

Think about a time when you disagreed or argued with someone. How did you try to resolve it? Write your answer on the lines below.

# READ

## Different Opinions

One beautiful thing about humans is that we are all different. No two humans have the exact same likes, dislikes, strengths, struggles, or opinions. People have different opinions about everything, from ice cream to laws. In the original Thirteen Colonies, many colonists disagreed with the king's laws and taxes, but others did not mind them. Why did some colonists think that some of the laws and taxes were unfair? Why did other colonists think that the laws and taxes were fair?

British tax laws raised tension in the colonies. Many colonists believed the taxes were unfair because they did not have representation in England's government. Remember that representation gives people a voice in how the government is run. Not having the opportunity to help make decisions in the government made many colonists angry. Some colonists, on the other hand, believed it was fair and good for the colonies to pay taxes. The taxes helped the British government protect the colonies from other countries who might try to attack them.

About one in six colonists were loyal to the king. These colonists, who were called **Loyalists,** felt comfortable with the king as their leader and liked being part of a powerful nation. The colonists who felt that the taxes and laws imposed on them by the British government were unfair were called **Patriots.** Later, these colonists would support declaring independence from Great Britain.

Discover! SOCIAL STUDIES • GRADE 4 • LESSON 14

## IN THE REAL WORLD

### Think About It

Colonists had different opinions about taxes in the colonies. Can you think of a rule that you and a sibling or a friend disagree on?

Human beings disagree all the time. If everyone agreed on everything, life might be really boring. It's ok to have different opinions, as long as people are respectful to one another. A good rule of thumb to remember when disagreeing with someone is to disagree with the idea rather than with the person.

# READ

## Colonists React

Almost half of the colonists were angry about taxes and were not afraid to do something about them. To show their disapproval of the king's laws, many colonists boycotted British goods. **Boycotting** was a protest in which people do not pay for or use a product or service. For example, when the king began taxing sugar, colonists stopped buying sugar from British sellers. This hurt those sellers' businesses, as well as the British government, because they were no longer making the same amount of money.

Another way colonists reacted to England's laws in the colonies was to **protest** them, or speak out against them. Colonists gathered in groups to voice their opinions and convince others that the taxes were unfair. Some made powerful speeches. Others chanted "no taxation without representation" in the streets. Many colonists protested taxes by refusing to pay them. These colonists were usually sent to jail. Sometimes the protests became violent.

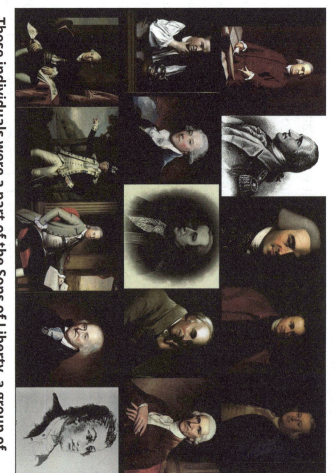

**These individuals were a part of the Sons of Liberty, a group of Patriots who protested Britain's taxes.**

*Sons of Liberty.jpg by several painters 18th century is in the public domain.*

## WRITE

Summarize two different ways colonists reacted to England's laws in the colonies.

............................................

............................................

............................................

............................................

............................................

............................................

............................................

# READ

## The Boston Massacre

The British Parliament sent more British soldiers to the colonies to keep peace and stop the protests. Since Boston had some of the largest protests, hundreds of soldiers were sent there to keep the peace. However, their presence only made things worse. Soon, the tensions increased to the point where physical fights between protesters and British soldiers were not unusual.

On March 5, 1770, an argument between a British soldier and a protester became worse as more protesters joined in and more soldiers arrived to stop the protesters. The protesters began throwing things, like stones, snowballs, and sticks at the soldiers. Some of the soldiers began firing their muskets into the crowd. Before it was done, five colonists were killed. This event became known as the Boston Massacre. The British called this event the "Incident on King Street" since that was the name of the street where it occurred.

After the Boston Massacre, there were different perspectives about what had happened and who was to blame. Many Loyalists believed that it was an unfortunate accident and that the soldiers were only trying to defend themselves. Many Patriots believed that the soldiers who fired into the crowd were guilty of murder.

When the soldiers were put on trial for murder, John Adams—a Patriot and future president—defended them. Adams argued that the soldiers felt that their lives were in danger and had defended themselves against an angry mob. In the end, four soldiers were found not guilty, and two were found guilty of a lesser charge and not punished severely. This increased the tensions in the colonies even more and helped lead to the American Revolution.

# REVIEW

In this lesson, you learned:

- People had different viewpoints of the Boston Massacre.
- Colonists felt differently about paying taxes to England.
- There were several different ways colonists reacted to England's laws in the colonies.

## Think About It

How do you think disagreements in the colonies, including having different perspectives of the Boston Massacre, affected tensions between colonists and Great Britain?

**Boston Massacre by Alonzo Chappel, 1878**

*BostonMassacre byAlonzoChappel1878.png by is in the public domain.*

# PRACTICE

Use the diagram below to compare and contrast the different viewpoints of events in the colonies, including taxes and the Boston Massacre. Write the similarities in the middle section and the differences in the two outer circles.

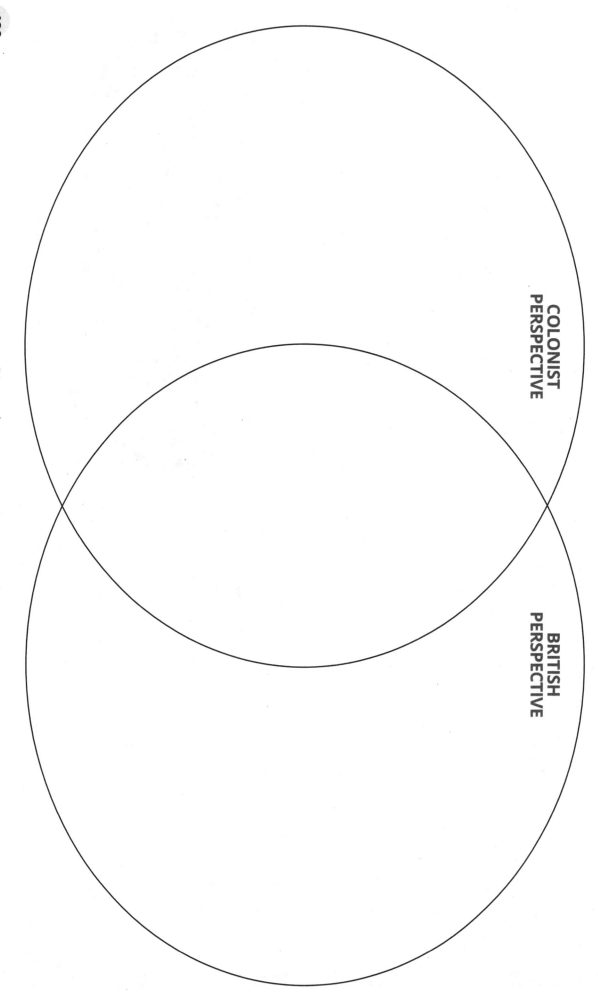

**COLONIST PERSPECTIVE**

**BRITISH PERSPECTIVE**

# SHOW WHAT YOU KNOW

Circle the correct phrase to complete each sentence.

1. Colonists reacted to England's laws in the colonies by _____.

A. boycotting British goods and protesting taxes

B. moving out of the colonies

C. changing their perspectives

2. Most colonists thought England's taxes were unfair. Those who disagreed thought taxes were fair because _____.

A. they got gifts from the king in exchange for taxes

B. they helped the British government protect the colonies

C. they had plenty of money to pay taxes

3. Angry colonists called the event on March 5, 1770 _____.

A. the Incident on King Street

B. Paul Revere's engraving

C. the Boston Massacre

4. British soldiers and people in England called the event on March 5, 1770 _____.

A. the Incident on King Street

B. Paul Revere's engraving

C. the Boston Massacre

# ONLINE CONNECTION

Find posters and images that were created after the Boston Massacre and show different perspectives of what happened. Remember that someone's perspective can include their opinion of something. For example, most colonists believed that the event was an attack on the colonists and that the British soldiers were to blame for the violent killings of five colonists. However, those you sided with Britain believed it was an unfortunate event or accident and that the British soldiers were defending themselves against an angry mob.

How do the images show the perspective of the artist? Discuss your ideas with your instructor or an adult.

5. Regarding the Boston Massacre, a British soldier or a loyalist might say _____.

A. the British soldiers were to blame, as they brutally killed five colonists

B. it was an accident and no one intended to shoot the colonists

6. Regarding the Boston Massacre, an angry colonist might say _____.

A. the British soldiers were to blame, as they brutally killed five colonists

B. it was an accident, and no one intended to shoot the colonists

# Lesson 15

## The Road to the Revolutionary War

**By the end of this lesson, you will be able to:**

- describe the Boston Tea Party and its results
- compare and contrast the Loyalists and Patriots
- summarize the reasons a colonist might choose to become a Loyalist or a Patriot

### Lesson Review

If you need to review the events leading up to the Boston Tea Party, please go to the lesson titled "The Boston Massacre."

### Academic Vocabulary

Read the following vocabulary words and definitions. Look through the lesson. Can you find each vocabulary word? Underline the vocabulary word in your lesson. Write the page number of where you found each word in the blanks.

- **boycott:** a protest in which people do not pay for or use a product or service (page ___)
- **levied:** to collect or raise by legal authority (page ___)
- **Loyalists:** colonists who supported Britain ruling the colonies (page ___)
- **monopoly:** total control over trade of a good or service (page ___)
- **Patriots:** colonists who supported the colonies having independence from Britain (page ___)
- **quarter:** using private property to feed and shelter the British military at will (page ___)
- **repealed:** taken back (page ___)

Throughout history, groups have sought the world's attention for causes they believed in. Look at this list of some of the most influential demonstrations in history:

- Ghandi's Salt March (India, 1930)
- The South African Defiance Campaign (South Africa, 1952)
- The March on Washington (US, 1963)
- The Delano Grape Strike (US, 1965–1970)

Research one of these events and write a paragraph explaining why you think it successfully captured the world's attention.

# EXPLORE

Think about a time that you needed to get someone's attention.

Maybe you had a big, exciting secret to share. Maybe you were trying to surprise someone. Maybe someone was about to get hurt and you wanted to prevent it. Maybe you were being ignored or upset and you needed it to stop.

That is how the Sons of Liberty felt when the British government charged higher and higher taxes, even though the colonists were not being represented in Parliament. As a result, they came up with a very creative plan to get not just the government's attention but also the attention of America's colonists.

Can you think of a situation where you would need to get someone's attention? What are creative ways you could get their attention in those situations? Write your ideas on the lines below.

...................................................................................................

...................................................................................................

...................................................................................................

...................................................................................................

...................................................................................................

...................................................................................................

...................................................................................................

...................................................................................................

## IN THE REAL WORLD

The Sons of Liberty destroyed a lot of tea, but what impact did this amount of tea have? To understand, you will need to stretch your math muscles!

The amount billed for the destroyed tea shipment at Boston Harbor was £9,659 in 1773. Today, it would be worth $989,395!

Now you can imagine how that got the attention of the British!

# READ

## Sons of Liberty Take Action

Tensions were building after the French and Indian War. The colonists had already tried resisting British taxes through **boycotts**, or protests in which people do not pay for or use a product or service. One group of colonists called the Sons of Liberty, led by Samuel Adams, had grown tired of having these disagreements over taxes. They decided something big needed to happen to show the British that these taxes would not be tolerated any longer.

They planned the Boston Tea Party. This was not a tea party with little sandwiches and teacups. Instead, under the cover of darkness in the middle of the night on December 16, 1773, the Sons of Liberty boarded ships full of tea docked in Boston Harbor. To hide their identities and avoid harsh or even deadly punishments, they disguised themselves as Mohawk Indians to symbolize their allegiance to America over Britain. They dumped the chests of tea into Boston Harbor, setting off a chain of events that eventually led to American independence.

**Illustration of Tea Being Destroyed at Boston Harbor**

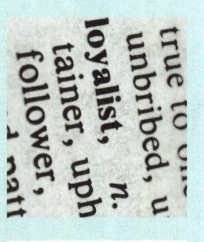

While the Sons of Liberty opposed British rule over the colonies, Loyalists continued to support Britain ruling the colonies. Even though the Loyalists did not agree with higher taxes or harsh laws, they believed in the ideas of natural rights and limited government. Most wanted to avoid mob rule and violence, so they supported more peaceful forms of protest. Some also had their businesses to consider.

Smaller groups of Loyalists had other reasons, such as Anglican clergy who believed the Church of England was the true church (with the king as its head). German immigrants liked that George III was of German heritage. Additionally, indentured servants and enslaved people were often promised freedom for loyalty.

# READ

## A Closer Look: The Tea Act of 1773

Why were the Sons of Liberty so upset with British rule anyway?

Britain **levied**, or raised and collected, a tax on tea in 1773. This added a fee that had to be paid to the only legal tea distributors in America—the British East India Company. The British government and monarchy had been supporting this company for almost 200 years. When the company fell on hard times, the government would enact laws and policies to funnel more business and money into the company. They were doing this to protect their investment in the company.

Many colonists, especially the Sons of Liberty, were strongly opposed to this because Parliament was ignoring laws of governing that would protect or benefit the colonies in many ways. But not only were the colonists being governed poorly, but they also had no representation in Parliament—or no one speaking for the rights and concerns of the colonists.

From this conflict came the expression, "No taxation without representation," meaning a people cannot be taxed if they have no say in the way they are governed. Colonists were being taxed to pay for the French and Indian War as well as to keep the British East India Company going. Many colonists began to feel like they were getting a raw deal.

Other colonists whose businesses depended on trade had reason to be upset with the **Patriots**, or colonists who supported independence from Britain. Not only did they destroy tea inventory, but they were also attracting attention that could negatively impact their ability to conduct business.

## TAKE A CLOSER LOOK

The British East India Company had a **monopoly**, or total control over trade of a good or service, in ports around the world. This meant colonists could only trade with Britain.

Patriots posed a threat to the livelihood of merchants trading goods that were delivered by the company. This was because merchants depended on the company for goods to sell or trade. Anything the Patriots did could hurt their business.

## READ

## British Response

The government had to respond to this display of resistance to British authority. Imagine being the king of the most powerful empire in the world. Would you allow colonists to openly disrespect your government in this way?

The king responded by passing laws known as the Intolerable Acts to punish the colonists for being openly defiant of the king. It began with increased military presence in the colonies—particularly Massachusetts—to help enforce the new provisions. The changes these laws made were:

- closing the Boston Port until the damaged tea had been paid for in full
- dismantling the local government of Massachusetts and installing British officials
- allowing British officials accused of crimes in the colonies to stand trial in England
- requiring colonists to **quarter** British soldiers, meaning the military could require the use of private property and force the owners to feed and shelter them at will

The colonists were very unhappy about these laws, largely because they punished all of the colonists without any opportunity to defend themselves in court instead of punishing just the Boston Tea Party participants.

## COLONISTS' RESPONSE

The colonists felt like they had to do something. The First Continental Congress convened, in which the colonies sent delegates to discuss what should be done about increasingly oppressive British rule. Twelve colonies were represented.

After much discussion, the Continental Congress chose to boycott all British goods to send a stronger message of their unhappiness with British rule.

## REVIEW

In this lesson, you learned:

- Britain levied a tax on tea in America, angering the colonists who felt that it was not acceptable to tax people who did not have representation in the government.
- Patriots in Boston rebelled by destroying a shipment of tea. The British government wrote the Intolerable Acts in response.
- The Continental Congress planned a boycott on British goods as a response to the Intolerable Acts.
- Colonists were torn over supporting British rule or American independence.

### Think About It

Would you have been a Loyalist or a Patriot? Why?

# PRACTICE

Create a persuasive advertisement in the box below to convince colonists to be either a Patriot or a Loyalist. Be sure to include reasons discussed in the lesson as to why someone would want to support your chosen side. Additionally, include at least one picture or sketch in your advertisement.

# SHOW WHAT YOU KNOW

Circle the correct answer for each question.

1. Why did the British pass the Tea Act?

A. to discourage all other beverages

B. to encourage tea drinking

C. to help the British East India Company keep going

D. to make tea their largest trade

2. What group led by Samuel Adams decided to take drastic action in response?

A. The British Resistance

B. Sons of Liberty

C. League of Women Voters

D. Daughters of the American Revolution

3. Which of these was not one of the Intolerable Act laws?

A. suspected Patriots got additional goods to sell at their businesses

B. forced quartering of soldiers

C. allowed accused British officials of standing trial in England instead of America

D. closed the Boston Port

4. What was the purpose of the Continental Congress?

A. to draft the Declaration of Independence

B. to draft an apology to King George III

C. to devise a response to the Intolerable Acts

D. to convince the colonists to remain loyal to Britain

## SHOW WHAT YOU KNOW

Evaluate each concern below and mark it with an L if it expresses a Loyalist concern or a P if it expresses a Patriot concern.

**5.** Britain's monopoly on trade limits my ability to trade freely with merchants from other countries. _____

**6.** My shipment of tea was destroyed by the Sons of Liberty. Now I have no tea to sell and no idea when I will be able to get more. _____

**7.** If we do not have anyone representing our interests and concerns in Parliament, how can they levy taxes on us? _____

**8.** I do not like the way I'm forced to do business because the British government leaves me little choice. But if I speak up, I could be charged with treason and imprisoned—or worse, hanged. _____

**9.** The king has dissolved our local government, putting in place his own chosen representatives to control us instead of representing our interests and concerns. _____

## ONLINE CONNECTION

Did you know that political cartoons were popular back in colonial America? Take a look at this popular cartoon from the era called *The Horse America Throwing Its Master.*

THE HORSE AMERICA, *throwing his Master.*

The rider represents King George III or Britain. The bucking horse represents America showing that they wanted to get out from under the unfair rule of Britain.

*The horse America, throwing his master. United States, 1779. Westminster: Pubd. by Wm. White, Aug. 1. Photograph. https://www.loc.gov/item/97514739/.*

# Declaration of Independence

**By the end of this lesson, you will be able to:**

- summarize and evaluate the parts of the Declaration of Independence

## Lesson Review

If you need to review events that happened before the Declaration of Independence, please go to the lesson titled "The Road to the Revolutionary War."

## Academic Vocabulary

Read the following vocabulary words and definitions. Look through the lesson. Can you find each vocabulary word? Underline the vocabulary word in your lesson. Write the page number of where you found each word in the blanks.

- **governance:** the ways a country or group chooses to run their government (page ___)

- **grievances:** complaints (page ___)

- **inalienable rights:** things people are allowed to do or have that cannot be taken away (page ___)

### IN THE REAL WORLD

As you learn about the Declaration of Independence in this lesson, consider how you might have written it if you were alive at that moment in time. After you complete the lesson, read the full text of the Declaration of Independence. You can find it at the National Archives online.

The language is old and very formal, so some words may seem confusing. If you need help, look up the definitions of unfamiliar words. Then, read the confusing parts aloud by inserting the definitions in place of the unfamiliar words.

The Founding Fathers depicted on the $2 bill.

# EXPLORE

Have you ever tried to convince a family member or friend to see things your way? How did you convince them to agree with you?

In the Declaration of Independence, the Founding Fathers weren't just airing their complaints against King George III. They were also making the case to their audience that not being ruled by Britain anymore was necessary (and that they had tried other options first).

When trying to persuade someone, you have to think about who you are speaking to and what would be convincing to them. That information should guide the points you make to persuade them.

Think of a time you were successful in convincing someone in your life to agree with you about something. How did you do it? Write about what happened on the lines below.

.................................................................................................
.................................................................................................
.................................................................................................
.................................................................................................
.................................................................................................
.................................................................................................
.................................................................................................
.................................................................................................
.................................................................................................

This statue depicts Thomas Jefferson, Benjamin Franklin, and John Adams (three of the Declaration's five authors) kneeling in prayer. It is located at Freedoms Foundation in Valley Forge, Pennsylvania.

# READ

## Seeking Separation from Britain

In the previous lesson, you learned about the tensions that caused Britain to go to war against the colonies. Many colonists thought it would be possible to come to an agreement with Britain. At the First Continental Congress in 1774, the Declaration of Rights and Grievances was written. **Grievances** are complaints, and this document listed complaints against King George III and Britain. The colonies wanted Britain to respect their rights. The colonies also thought they should not be taxed when they did not have anyone representing them in the British government.

Others knew this would not convince the king to respect the colonists' right to have a say in their own **governance**, or the ways the country chose to run their government. They were proven right when King George III did not change how the colonists were being treated.

It became clear that an agreement with the British government would not be possible. During the Second Continental Congress in 1776, the Lee Resolution called for an official separation from Britain. This was a heated topic for Congress, as most colonies were against independence at the time. They voted to delay discussion on it for three weeks.

During that time, Congress appointed the Committee of Five to draft a document that would announce what the colonies would do if the Lee Resolution passed. The members were Benjamin Franklin, John Adams, Robert R. Livingston, Roger Sherman, and Thomas Jefferson.

This was scary for the colonists, as they had to walk a very thin line. Breaking away from Britain could be seen as treason—punishable by death! Additionally, with a much smaller army and far fewer resources, the chances of the colonies winning a war against Britain were slim.

The number of Patriots—or people who sought independence from Britain—continued to rise as separation from Britain became a more serious matter. For the Patriots, liberty truly was a matter of life or death. If they were caught, the Patriots would be tried for treason and risked execution. This was a dangerous gamble each Patriot took, especially the 56 signers of the Declaration of Independence.

That is why they ended the document with these lines: "And for the support of this Declaration, with a firm reliance on the protection of divine Providence, we mutually pledge to each other our Lives, our Fortunes and our sacred Honor." These men pledged everything in order to bring about the independence of our nation.

LIBERTY OR DEATH

**The Patriots had to choose between liberty or death. Which would you choose?**

# READ

## Parts of the Declaration

Even though Thomas Jefferson is considered the writer of the Declaration of Independence, the four other members of the Committee of Five helped to decide what was written. On July 4, 1776, the Declaration of Independence was signed by the Second Continental Congress. This meant the colonies were rejecting Britain's rule over them.

**Imagine writing such an important document with a feather pen!**

There are four parts of the Declaration of Independence.

**Preamble:** This section explains why the document was being written. It says that sometimes it is necessary for people to separate from a government, like when they are not being treated fairly or their rights are being ignored. The writers wanted people to know the reasons that the colonies were declaring their independence.

**Declaration of Natural Rights:** This section lists the rights that every person has that cannot be taken away or threatened. When these rights are threatened or taken away, the declaration says that people can change or create a new government. These **inalienable** rights are: life, liberty, and the pursuit of happiness.

**Bill (List) of Grievances:** This section lists the grievances the colonists had against King George III. The colonists did not like that they were treated differently than British citizens. They had to pay heavy taxes, and Britain controlled a lot of their economy, including trade. British armies could also be aggressive to the colonists, and many colonists were forced to house them in their homes.

**Resolution of Independence:** This section officially declares the colonies independent from Britain. They had asked Britain to treat the colonies better, but King George III refused to do so. Therefore, the colonists felt they had to declare themselves independent from British rule.

## WRITE

Imagine being a colonist during this time. Write one reason the colonies should stay loyal to Britain and one reason they should want independence.

| One reason to stay loyal was... | One reason to be independent was... |
|---|---|
| | |
| | |
| | |
| | |
| | |

# PRACTICE

In your own words, write or draw pictures to summarize what was written in each section of the Declaration of Independence in the chart below.

| Preamble | Declaration of Natural Rights |
|---|---|
| **Bill (List) of Grievances** | **Resolution of Independence** |

Not all colonists felt confident in going against Britain. Some colonies' representatives at the Second Continental Congress needed to be convinced that declaring independence was the right decision. Why do you think representatives may have felt uncertain about declaring independence?

# REVIEW

In this lesson, you learned:

- The Declaration of Independence was written to declare the colonies' independence from Britain. It was signed on July 4, 1776.

- The Declaration of Independence has four parts: Preamble, Declaration of Natural Rights, Bill (List) of Grievances, and Resolution of Independence.

**Think About It**

How do you think this document has influenced the course of world history since 1776?

## IN THE REAL WORLD

What is your absolute least enjoyable chore? What don't you like about it?

Whether it's making your bed or sweeping the floor, you get to pretend for a moment that you're declaring yourself independent from ever doing it again!

Imagine you are declaring your independence from that chore. Write a letter to your parents explaining why you shouldn't be expected to do it any longer.

## SHOW WHAT YOU KNOW

Match each summary below to the section of the Declaration of Independence it describes.

1. _____ A list of things King George III had done to go against the colonists' rights and treat them unfairly.

2. _____ This section explains why the colonies are making this declaration, including that they had decided to separate from Britain and wanted to explain their reasons.

3. _____ This lists the inalienable rights that all people have. These rights are life, liberty, and the pursuit of happiness.

4. _____ This concludes the declaration by stating that the colonies have tried to reach an agreement with Britain, but Britain has refused. Due to this, the colonies must announce their independence from Britain.

A. Preamble

B. Declaration of Natural Rights

C. Bill (List) of Grievances

D. Resolution of Independence

5. Write a three-sentence summary of the Bill (List) of Grievances.

...........................................................................................................

...........................................................................................................

...........................................................................................................

...........................................................................................................

# Major Revolutionary War Battles

**By the end of this lesson, you will be able to:**

- identify on a timeline major events that led to the British colonies' independence from England
- identify important battles of the Revolutionary War, including identifying who won the battle
- describe the Battle of Yorktown and its importance in ending the Revolutionary War

## Lesson Review

If you need to review the events that led to the Revolutionary War, please go to the lesson titled "The Road to the Revolutionary War."

## Academic Vocabulary

Read the following vocabulary words and definitions. Look through the lesson. Can you find each vocabulary word? Underline the vocabulary word in your lesson. Write the page number of where you found each word in the blanks.

- **fortifying:** adding protection to a place to defend it from attack (page ___)
- **tactical:** carefully planned actions to achieve a military goal or result (page ___)
- **turning point:** a moment when an important change occurs that has an impact on the outcome of an event (page ___)

# ONLINE CONNECTION

This lesson explores several major battles of the Revolutionary War. As you learn about these events, imagine yourself as an observer or even a participant in one of these battles.

On the sites where these battles occurred, groups of people called reenactors devote to keeping the memory of history alive by performing for thousands of people each year.

Look up a video of a battle reenactment. What difference does it make to see the battle taking place when it originally occurred? Write a paragraph about how seeing the reenactment influenced your understanding of the event.

# EXPLORE

*...It is in vain for me to think of telling you News, because you have direct Intelligence from Ticonderoga much sooner than I have, and from N. York sooner than I can transmit it to you...*

– Letter from John Adams to James Warren, Sep. 4, 1776

In today's world, we can know what is happening on the other side of the world as it happens! Thanks to technology, we are more connected than ever before.

During the Revolutionary War, it was much harder to get information to people that were not in the same place. In August 1776, John Adams was living in Boston, Massachusetts. At that same time, James Warren was the paymaster general for the Continental Congress in Philadelphia, Pennsylvania.

Warren had access to the messengers and spies working for the Continental Army. Even though Adams was closer to the areas engaged in battle at that time, he did not have the communication network Warren did. Warren could find out from his spies and messengers what was happening a lot faster than Adams could.

How do you think a delay in receiving communications or information could affect a battle? Write your ideas on the lines below.

...........................................................................................

...........................................................................................

...........................................................................................

...........................................................................................

...........................................................................................

...........................................................................................

## TAKE A CLOSER LOOK

The Pennsylvania rifle, also known as the American longrifle, was the preferred weapon for American sharpshooters. This gun is considered a crucial factor in the Continental Army's success. British rifles were incredibly accurate to within 100 feet (31 meters). However, the Pennsylvania rifle was accurate within 300 feet (91 meters). The longer range made it possible for sharpshooters to successfully hit targets from a much greater distance.

# READ

## A War Begins

Let's look at some of the battles of the Revolutionary War.

### THE BATTLES OF LEXINGTON & CONCORD (APRIL 19, 1775)

This is where the first shot of the war was fired. People often refer to this shot as the "shot heard 'round the world." Although the Patriots fell back at Lexington, they returned to Concord and defeated the British army. This win was likely due to the advance warning from Paul Revere's (and other riders') midnight ride that the British were coming.

### THE BATTLE OF BUNKER HILL (JUNE 17, 1775)

At this battle, the British defeated the Patriots, taking Boston Harbor in a **tactical**, or carefully planned, victory. After this turning point, going back under British rule was no longer an option for the colonies. King George III responded with the Proclamation of Rebellion in August.

### THE BATTLE OF SULLIVAN'S ISLAND (JUNE 28, 1776)

Just weeks before the signing of the Declaration of Independence, the Patriots were able to fend off the British army. They seized Charleston Harbor by **fortifying**, or reinforcing, the small Sullivan's Island. This was key to successfully blocking the channel into Charleston Harbor and preventing the British from making landfall. As a result, this delayed the British from reaching important southern ports for three years. Had Charleston been lost so early in the war, the story would have been very different.

**Old North Bridge** where the "shot heard 'round the world" was originally fired.

**Example of an officer's quarters at battle encampments.**

# READ

## Fighting for Independence

After the Declaration of Independence was signed, the stakes were raised even higher for the Patriots. Patriot Patrick Henry famously said, "Give me liberty or give me death!" when recruiting militia members in Virginia. Although this statement expressed a popular feeling for Patriots at the time, it was also a very literal situation they faced with fighting the British.

### THE BATTLE OF LONG ISLAND (AUGUST 27, 1776)

The British served the Patriots their first post-Declaration defeat in a battle on Long Island. This forced Washington to retreat to Brooklyn and eventually out of New York into New Jersey. The British controlled New York City for the entirety of the war from that point on.

### THE BATTLE OF TRENTON (DECEMBER 26, 1776)

The Patriots suffered a number of defeats in New York and New Jersey. By the end of 1776, the ragtag Patriot army was on the verge of collapse. Over Christmas, Washington surprised his men with an ambitious plan to cross the Delaware River overnight and ambush Hessian troops—German troops the British hired—stationed on the other side.

*Washington Crossing the Delaware by Emanuel Leutze, MMA-NYC, 1851.jpg by Emanuel Leutze is in the public domain.*

Conditions on the Delaware were so dangerous that two units were unable to make the crossing, leaving the Patriots with fewer men than were planned. Still, the Patriots managed to defeat the British by surrounding the Hessians and forcing their surrender. This raised the soldiers' spirits and increased the number of people signing up to join the army.

## IN THE REAL WORLD

When possible, cannons were used during many battles.

**American Revolution Cannons at Yorktown, VA**

**Canon on the Field at Saratoga National Park**

# READ

## An Alliance Is Forged

### THE BATTLES OF SARATOGA (SEPTEMBER–OCTOBER 1777)

The British army intended to separate New England from the southern states. This plan failed when they were surrounded by Patriots in this battle that proved to be a major turning point in the war.

After this victory, other countries began to offer aid and support. France was the first. Although they had been secretly sending supplies as early as June 1775, they did not sign the Treaty of Alliance until 1778. This committed France to sending money, supplies, and troops to aid the Continental Army.

The Surrender of General Burgoyne at Saratoga October 16 1777.jpeg by John Trumball is in the public domain.

### THE SIEGE OF CHARLESTON (MARCH–MAY 1780)

After significant losses in the north and abandoning Philadelphia by 1778, the British renewed their focus on seizing southern ports. They finally succeeded in winning control of Charleston Harbor after failing in 1776.

### THE SIEGE OF YORKTOWN (SEPTEMBER–OCTOBER 1781)

Although the British army was plentiful in number, they had been run completely ragged by their campaign in South Carolina. They retreated to Yorktown. An incoming French fleet landed at the Chesapeake Bay while the French and Continental Armies on land began their march to Virginia. Along the way, they convinced the British army they were planning a siege in New York. Continental troops led by Marquis de Lafayette trailed the British in Virginia to stay aware of their movements. All of the units met in Yorktown without the British knowing. With the combined armies fighting under the leadership of George Washington, they forced General Lord Cornwallis to surrender, effectively ending the war.

# WRITE

Which battle do you think was most important in the Revolutionary War? Why?

# PRACTICE

Use the words in the Word Bank to identify which battles are being describe below.

**Word Bank:**
The Battle of Bunker Hill    The Battle of Trenton
The Siege of Charleston     The Battles of Saratoga
The Battle of Sullivan's Island   The Siege of Yorktown
The Battle of Long Island   The Battles of Lexington & Concord

1. This battle was the turning point in which making peace with Britain was no longer possible. _____

2. This battle ensured Britain finally gained control of an important southern port. _____

3. After this victory, foreign countries were willing to send aid and support to the Americans. _____

4. After a string of losses and several retreats, the Americans delivered a surprising loss to the British in this battle, boosting the spirits of the soldiers. _____

5. As the first engagement of the Revolutionary War, people will refer to this battle as the "shot heard 'round the world." _____

6. This battle forced Washington to retreat out of New York into New Jersey, giving Britain full control of New York City. _____

7. The Patriots blocked Britain's control of a major harbor and several major ports during this battle. _____

8. The French and Continental Armies forced General Lord Cornwallis to surrender and end the war at this battle. _____

# REVIEW

In this lesson, you learned:

- The American and British armies both experienced major wins and losses during the Revolutionary War.

- There were several turning points, like Bunker Hill (ending the hope of peace with Britain) and Saratoga (a victory that convinced foreign powers to aid the cause of American independence).

- The war was finally won by the Americans in 1781 at Yorktown, when the tactical efforts of the American–French alliance forced General Lord Cornwallis to surrender.

## Think About It
Do you think the Patriots would have won at Yorktown without help from the French? Why or why not?

## WHAT SHOW YOU KNOW

Identify the winner of each battle listed below.

1. The Battles of Lexington & Concord

2. The Battle of Bunker Hill

3. The Battle of Sullivan's Island

4. The Battle of Long Island

5. The Battle of Trenton

6. The Battles of Saratoga

7. The Siege of Charleston

8. The Siege of Yorktown

9. What are two reasons the Americans were victorious at Yorktown?

1. ....................................................................................................

2. ....................................................................................................

## CREATE

At the beginning of this lesson, you considered how hard it would be to get information quickly at this time in history. Newspapers gave people a way to get information in a relatively short amount of time.

Imagine you are a newspaper writer, and the messenger has just arrived with the news that the British have surrendered. How would you take on the task of delivering the story of a lifetime?

Write your own front page story about the event.

# Lesson 18

# People and Symbols of the Revolution

## By the end of this lesson, you will be able to:

- identify key people of the Revolutionary time period
- explain how elements of the United States flag design represent the 13 colonies
- identify Flag Day as a holiday celebrated in the United States

## Academic Vocabulary

Read the following vocabulary words and definitions. Look through the lesson. Can you find each vocabulary word? Underline the vocabulary word in your lesson. Write the page number of where you found each word in the blanks.

- **apocryphal:** a story that cannot be proven true but is widely told as if it is and is based in real events (page ____)

- **symbols:** things that represent or stand for something else (page ____)

PLAY

Do you see yourself as a general, like George Washington? Maybe you see yourself good at leading a cause, like John Adams? Are you great at a lot of things, like politician/philosopher/scientist/inventor/diplomat Benjamin Franklin?

After the lesson, write a speech that the famous Revolutionary War–era figure of your choice might give at one of the following occasions:

- to motivate and reassure the troops after a loss in battle
- to congratulate soldiers returning from Yorktown in Congress
- to celebrate the Patriots' victory at a town's public house

Now get creative and dress up like your chosen person as you deliver your speech.

# EXPLRE

**Symbols** are things that represent or stand for something else. In this lesson, you will learn about some of the symbols of the American Revolution. However, we encounter symbols in our daily lives as well!

Some common symbols we see regularly include:

🍀 Four-leaf clover: this symbolizes luck

🛒 Shopping cart icon: this symbolizes a link to an online shopping cart where a shopper can "check out" and complete their purchase

🛑 Stop sign: this symbolizes "stop" in various settings

⏻ Power: this symbolizes power, usually located on on/off buttons on remotes and devices

Take a look at the American flag below. A flag is a symbol of a country's identity, it's history, or what it is proud of. What do you think the stars, stripes, and colors in the American flag symbolize?

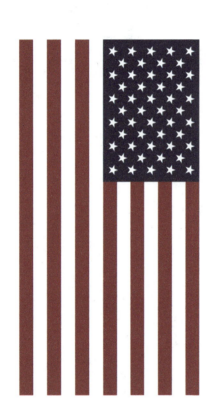

# READ

## Important People of the Revolutionary War

There were many important figures during the Revolutionary War—too many to name here! Below are some of those people and what they are known for.

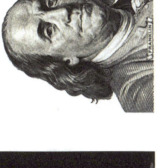

### JOHN ADAMS

As part of the Committee of Five, Adams hand-selected Thomas Jefferson to be the Declaration of Independence's main author. He was also elected the second US president.

### ABIGAIL ADAMS

As the wife of John Adams, Abigail Adams was an intelligent and trusted advisor to her husband. Her many letters give us insight into the important role of women in the early US. She believed women should have property rights and the right to an education, as well as believed slavery was evil.

### BENJAMIN FRANKLIN

As part of the Committee of Five, Franklin is credited with developing the US Post Office, negotiating the Treaty of Paris, and inventing many things.

### GEORGE WASHINGTON

Even though he was general of the Continental army and the first president of the US, Washington disliked political factions (or parties) and worked hard to maintain neutrality.

### BENEDICT ARNOLD

Although he was an American general, Arnold's name became a synonym for "traitor" due to working with the British army to negotiate a Continental army surrender in a battle at West Point.

# READ

## Important People of the Revolutionary War (cont.)

Here are some more important people from the American Revolution.

### MOLLY PITCHER

Although her true name remains uncertain, Pitcher delivered water to soldiers and to cool down cannons on the field. When her husband died in a battle at Monmouth, she took over his cannon.

### MARQUIS DE LAFAYETTE

Although originally from France, Lafayette became major-general in the Continental Army. He made several trips to France to ask for aid and French support for the Patriots.

### SAMUEL ADAMS

As a cousin to John Adams, Samuel Adams organized the Boston Tea Party and other acts of resistance against British taxation. Adams was also a signer of the Declaration of Independence.

### ALEXANDER HAMILTON

Although he was an immigrant from the Caribbean island of Nevis, Hamilton was a secretary to General Washington during the war. He founded the *New York Post* newspaper and served as the first US Secretary of the Treasury.

### THOMAS JEFFERSON

Apart from his role as the main author of the Declaration of Independence, Jefferson was the governor of Virginia and later the US ambassador to France. He served as vice president under John Adams and was elected the third president of the US.

# WRITE

Identify one person that you had never heard of before from this lesson, what you learned about them, and why you think they were important to the American Revolution.

# READ

## Symbolism in the US Flag

Another important person of this time period is Betsy Ross, although her story is **apocryphal**—or cannot be proven true but is widely told as if it is and is based in real events.

When a design for the original flag was being worked on, Betsy Ross had the idea to use five-point stars instead of six. George Washington preferred it so much that, he gave her the go-ahead to make the flag.

In reality, it was likely a group effort that underwent several changes in the design process. The first official government record of the flag's design came when the flag was approved by Congress on June 14, 1777. That day is still celebrated today as Flag Day! On Flag Day each year, people put out flags on their homes and businesses. Some towns even hold parades or other activities to celebrate the flag that symbolizes our nation.

The 13 stripes on the American flag today represent the 13 colonies. There were also 13 stars on the first flag that represented the colonies, but now there are 50 stars to represent all 50 states. The color white in the stripes represents innocence and the red represents valour and courage. The blue behind the stars represents justice.

**This Flag Is Still Known as the Betsy Ross Flag**

# REVIEW

In this lesson, you learned:

- There were many people who did amazing, noteworthy things to support American independence.

- Even though we often hear about the Founding Fathers, there were women in important roles as well, like Abigail Adams and Molly Pitcher.

- The flag is full of symbolism, from its colors to the design and placement of the stars.

- The day the flag became official was June 14, 1777. We celebrate Flag Day on June 14 each year.

## Think About It

If you had been alive at the time, how do you think you would have contributed to the founding of our nation?

# PRACTICE

Have you ever collected trading cards, such as baseball cards, football cards, or cards from a popular game where imaginary creatures battle each other? The people you studied today seem like they are important enough to have trading cards too.

In the boxes below, create a trading card for one important person in the American Revolution. In the box labeled "Front of the Trading Card," draw a picture to show something important about them and write their name. In the box labeled "Back of the Trading Card," write important facts about the person.

**FRONT OF THE TRADING CARD**

**BACK OF THE TRADING CARD**

## SHOW WHAT YOU KNOW

Answer the following questions with the name of the important person.

**Word Bank:**

| | | |
|---|---|---|
| Abigail Adams | George Washington | John Adams | Benjamin Franklin |
| Benedict Arnold | Alexander Hamilton | Molly Pitcher | |
| Samuel Adams | Thomas Jefferson | Marquis de LaFayette | |

1. I was a trusted advisor to the second president of the US. _____

2. My name is now a synonym for "traitor" because I tried negotiating a surrender with the British army. _____

3. I organized resistance actions against several tax laws imposed in the colonies, including the Boston Tea Party. _____

4. Even though I was general of the Continental Army, I disliked political factions and worked hard to maintain neutrality. _____

5. As the first Secretary of the Treasury, I set up our nation's financial systems. _____

6. I was the main author of the Declaration of Independence. _____

7. I was the second president of the US and hand-picked the author of the Declaration of Independence. _____

8. After my husband died on the field at Monmouth, I took over his cannon. _____

9. I was a valuable member of the Continental Army even though I came from France. _____

10. I developed the US Postal Service and negotiated the Treaty of Paris. _____

# SHOW WHAT YOU KNOW

Fill in the blanks with the correct words.

**11.** The red and white stripes symbolize the 13 _____.

**12.** Today, there are 50 _____ on the flag instead of 13.

**13.** _____ is a holiday celebrated in the US on June 14.

# IN THE REAL WORLD

A flag is usually made of symbols that are meaningful for a group or place—like how the US flag has used colors and numbers to represent the union of the states.

Select a flag from another country that is different from the US flag. Research the history of that flag and what it symbolizes. Write a paragraph explaining the details you discovered before drawing the flag in careful detail.

# Chapter 2 Review

## By the end of this lesson, you will:

- review the information from the lessons in Chapter 2, "A New Country."

## Lesson Review

Throughout the chapter, we have learned the following big ideas:

- France and Britain went to war over the Ohio River Valley. (Lesson 11)

- Having won the war, Britain gained a lot of land in North America while conditions improved for American colonists. Indigenous tribes who were aligned with France suffered after the war. (Lesson 12)

- The war was very expensive, and the British tried to make the colonists pay for it through multiple tax acts that the colonists did not like and pushed back against. (Lesson 13)

- Tensions over taxation without representation led to protests—one of the biggest being in Boston. Britain sent troops to control the protests, but that only made the tensions worse. This resulted in the Boston Massacre. (Lesson 14)

- The colonists largely grew tired of continued taxation, lack of governance, and military presence from Britain. The Boston Tea Party led to Britain passing the Intolerable Acts, starting the domino effect that began the Revolutionary War. (Lesson 15)

- The Declaration of Independence stated the colonies' desire to become independent from Britain. (Lesson 16)

- The Revolutionary War began with battles at Lexington & Concord and ended with General Cornwallis surrendering at Yorktown. (Lesson 17)

- Many notable people contributed in important ways to the fight for American independence. (Lesson 18)

Go back and review the lessons as needed while you complete the activities.

## IN THE REAL WORLD

Patriot soldiers fought through harsh conditions, lack of food and other resources, and opposition from friends, family, and neighbors. Still, these brave soldiers put their lives on the line to secure our freedom.

You have learned about battles in which the soldiers were lacking morale and needed a boost—like The Battle of Trenton. Did you know you can be a big morale boost to those currently serving your country overseas?

There are many organizations that can connect you to a soldier who might like a kind word from a new friend. Look online or in your community to find out how you can write to a soldier stationed far away from home.

# REVIEW

## Tensions Building

Even though the end of the French and Indian War relieved tensions in the colonies, Britain's decision to hold the colonies financially responsible for the cost of the war created new tensions between colonists and the British government. These are the tensions that eventually led to American independence as a result of the Revolutionary War.

Initially, the colonists protested new taxes and boycotted the taxed items. The British government responded in ways that showed compromise, like repealing the Sugar and Stamp Acts. However, Britain continued to treat the colonies unfairly. When they felt that someone needed to push back on Britain, the Sons of Liberty organized the Boston Tea Party. As a result, Britain wanted to show the colonists their authority and passed the Intolerable Acts, making life very difficult in the colonies.

The colonists refused to back down and began organizing their own government through the Continental Congresses. They attempted to negotiate peace with Britain, but the battles between the two countries began at Lexington & Concord.

After the Battle of Bunker Hill, the course for war was set. The Second Continental Congress signed the Declaration of Independence and paved the path toward American independence.

# TAKE A CLOSER LOOK

A revolution was far from the minds of most American colonists at the time of the Boston Massacre. Tensions were mounting, and this event increased anger at the British government. Yet it is important to remember that the colonists' main complaint at this point in time was being taxed without representation. The colonists wanted to feel like they had a voice in their own governance.

# WRITE

Select an event below. In one or two sentences, speculate (imagine and guess) the outcome if the event happened differently.

Events: French and Indian War, Boston Massacre, Second Continental Congress, Battles at Saratoga, Siege of Yorktown

# REVIEW

## Important People and Places

It was not clear to the colonists when the French and Indian War ended that the British taxation and governance that followed would be more than they could handle. Although we can now see how events built on each other as they lead up to the American Revolution, people were simply responding to their circumstances the best they could.

Look at the timeline below to review major battles of the American Revolution, when they happened, and which side won.

# REVIEW

Did you remember these important people of the Revolution? What is one thing you remember about each of them?

- Abigail Adams
- Benedict Arnold
- Samuel Adams
- George Washington
- Alexander Hamilton
- Thomas Jefferson
- John Adams
- Molly Pitcher
- Marquis de Lafayette
- Benjamin Franklin

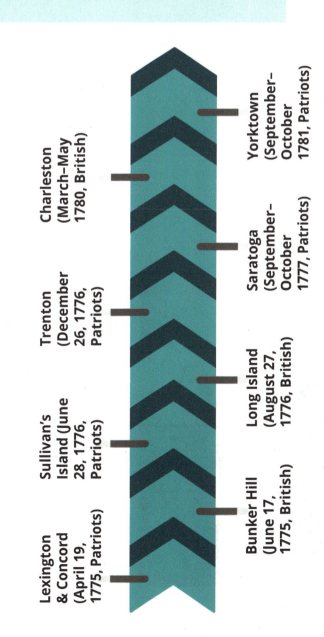

**Lexington & Concord** (April 19, 1775, Patriots)

**Bunker Hill** (June 17, 1775, British)

**Sullivan's Island** (June 28, 1776, Patriots)

**Long Island** (August 27, 1776, British)

**Trenton** (December 26, 1776, Patriots)

**Saratoga** (September–October 1777, Patriots)

**Charleston** (March–May 1780, British)

**Yorktown** (September–October 1781, Patriots)

# PRACTICE

## Visualizing Vocabulary

Draw a picture of each word to help you remember its meaning.

| boycott | Loyalists |
|---|---|
| **Patriots** | **fortifying** |
| **inalienable rights** | **grievances** |

Many of your vocabulary words in this chapter contain common word roots. Spotting and understanding common word roots helps to decode and understand unfamiliar terms. Here are examples of word roots in your Chapter 2 vocabulary:

- **monopoly:** This word is made up of two Greek roots: *mono* and *polein. Mono* means "one," and *polein* means "to sell."

- **fortify:** The Latin root *fortis* means "to make strong."

- **repeal:** This word is made up of two French root words: the root *re* meaning "back" and the root *apeler* meaning to "call."

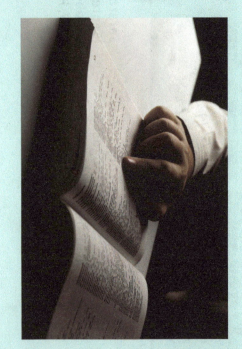

# PRACTICE

## Check the Temperature

Think about the list of major events listed below. Which events had higher or lower tension? Events with higher tension would have caused a lot of people to get upset or even fight. Events with lower tension would mean that people were more calm and at peace. Place each event in the list under the thermometer you think represents the tension level that event caused.

Events: Boycotts, Boston Massacre, Intolerable Acts, Boston Tea Party, Declaring Independence

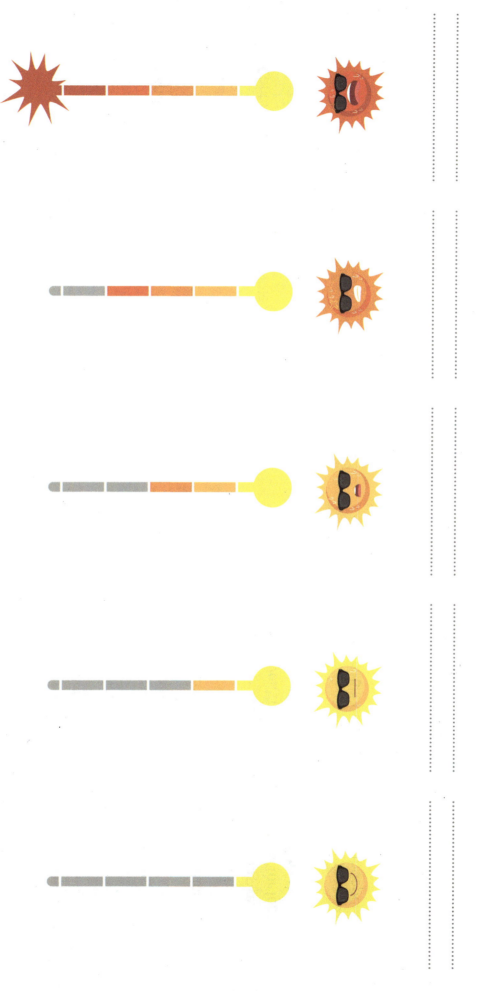

# PRACTICE

## What's the Link?

For each pair of terms below, explain how they are related.

**1.** George Washington, John Adams

........................................................................

**2.** Samuel Adams, Boston Tea Party

........................................................................

........................................................................

**3.** Sugar and Stamp Acts, boycotts

........................................................................

........................................................................

**4.** First Continental Congress, Intolerable Acts

........................................................................

........................................................................

**5.** Abigail Adams, John Adams

........................................................................

........................................................................

**6.** Inalienable rights, Declaration of Independence

........................................................................

........................................................................

**SHOW WHAT YOU KNOW**

Think about what you've learned about in this chapter. Circle how you feel:

4 – I know this chapter really well. I could teach it to someone.

3 – I know this chapter pretty well.

2 – I am still learning this chapter. I am not sure about some things.

1 – I am confused. I have a lot of questions about what I've learned.

Talk to your instructor about your answers. When you're ready, ask your instructor for the Show What You Know activity for the chapter.

**WRITE**

Think about your learning. What stands out to you in the lessons? What questions do you have? What do you wonder about? You can use this page to take notes, write out your responses, and then discuss them with your instructor.

# Chapter 3
# The Constitution

My friend! It's me, Monty, the hug-loving lion. The last time we talked, I told you about the sea voyage I took with Maria and my best friend, Leo. We didn't like the crew on our ship, the Sea Urchin. They were mean and didn't like hugs! But it turns out there were some great folks on the ship.

The passengers on the Sea Urchin were much nicer than the crew. Thank goodness! I met Professor Tibbs one evening on the deck. He teaches American History! What a pleasant surprise.

I am very curious, and I wanted to know everything about the United States of America. I asked Professor Tibbs, "If I could read one thing to know the most about the United States, what should I read?"

"Read this, young lion friend," he said. He reached down and took a pamphlet out of his pocket. It was a lot shorter than I expected. It said the Constitution of the United States. It was a little book of rules. The Founding Fathers who wrote it wanted US citizens to have laws that protected freedom and created a government that works.

The Constitution inspired me to be a better leader in my kingdom. Trust me; I'm not lyin'!

## What Will I Learn?

This chapter focuses on how the US Constitution was created. It includes an overview of the Articles of Confederation and how the Constitution was written and ratified.

## Lessons at a Glance

# Lesson 20

# Articles of Confederation

## By the end of this lesson, you will be able to:

- describe the reason the Continental Congress wanted to create a plan for the country's government
- define the word *confederation* and relate it to the states in the new country
- identify the purpose of the Articles of Confederation
- summarize the problems with the Articles of Confederation
- explain why the Articles of Confederation did not give enough power to the federal government

## Lesson Review

If you need to review the earliest form of government in America, please go to the lesson titled "Plymouth Colony."

## Academic Vocabulary

Review the following vocabulary words and their meanings. Look through the lesson. Can you find each vocabulary word? Underline the vocabulary word in your lesson. Write the page number of where you found each word in the blanks.

- **Articles of Confederation:** a document that outlined a plan for the American government and power that federal and state governments had (page ___)
- **confederation:** colonies or states coming together for a common cause (page ___)
- **Congress:** a group of representatives from different colonies that make decisions for the whole country (page ___)
- **constitution:** a document that explains the rules and responsibilities of the government and how it should be run (page ___)

- **Continental Congress:** a group of people who got together to represent each colony and make decisions (page ___)
- **federal government:** leaders, laws, and rules that apply to all of the states in a country (page ___)
- **legislative branch:** the part of government that defines how Congress makes laws (page ___)
- **state government:** a government with leaders and laws in one individual state (page ___)
- **treaties:** agreements between countries or people (page ___)

### IN THE REAL WORLD

Remember when the Pilgrims signed the Mayflower Compact and promised to follow the rules and laws of their colony? This set of rules and laws helped everyone work together to be successful. Any group that has to work together, including in communities, businesses, and families, follows rules to be successful. This is also true for each of the United States. States must have rules to be able to work together. People in each state have to follow the rules and laws.

What are some laws in your state? Talk about a few examples with your instructor.

# EXPLORE

## Play by the Rules

Have you ever played chess before? If so, think back to a time when you didn't know how to play. Imagine you and a friend are sitting down to play chess, but neither one of you knows the rules and you're not allowed to talk about them before you start playing. What might happen when you try to start playing? What could go wrong? Stop and think about how playing this game might be difficult or discuss these questions with your instructor.

Why is it more fun to play games when everyone knows and follows the rules? Write at least three reasons or give specific examples to answer this question on the lines below.

Drafting the Articles of Confederation

York Town, Pennsylvania  1777  13¢ USA

What do you think is happening in the drawing on the stamp? It shows leaders signing the Articles of Confederation. The Articles of Confederation were similar to a list of rules for a game, but the rules were about how the United States would be run.

# READ

## A Need for Rules

Have you ever gone to a friend's house who has a different set of rules than you? Were you able to behave in ways that are not allowed in your home, or were the rules more strict? Whether you are at a friend's house or out in the community, rules help keep you safe. In the United States, some rules are defined in the Constitution. A **constitution** is a document that provides a plan for how the government of a country should be run. It can also explain the rights and responsibilities of citizens and the government.

The Constitution of the United States still defines responsibilities and rights today, but it didn't exist until 1787. Before that, colonists created a different set of rules to define their government. It was called the Articles of Confederation.

When the 13 colonies became independent states separate from England, they needed to form their own government and have their own rules. The 13 colonies formed a **confederation**, or a group of states with common goals. Leaders from each state met to make decisions about important topics, including how the government would work. This group was called the **Continental Congress**. The goal of the Continental Congress was to create a plan for the government of their new country. The document they drafted, which defined the new government, was the **Articles of Confederation**. If you created a brand-new government, what laws would you create?

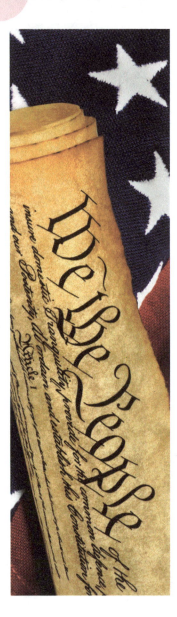

## IN THE REAL WORLD

Rules and laws are important. They help groups of people work better together. What are some laws we follow in our communities?

- Adults follow the speed limit when driving.
- We throw trash away instead of littering.

# READ

## Rules and Laws for the New Country

The Articles of Confederation included a plan for a government and rules about what the federal and state governments could and could not do. The **federal government** had some power, including the ability to make **treaties**—or agreements with other countries—and start wars. But most of the powers belonged to the individual states. This would be like the kids of your house having a lot of power and the parents having very little. How do you think that would work?

**State governments** were given a lot of freedom to make laws that worked for themselves. They each made their own form of money and charged different amounts of taxes—money given to the government—to their citizens. The federal government couldn't collect taxes or tell states to use a certain type of money.

Under the Articles of Confederation, it was as if each of the states were operating as their own mini-nation rather than working together as a country. This made the Articles of Confederation really unsuccessful for the new country. Think about a time you tried something you thought would work well but was unsuccessful. What did you try? Why didn't it work? What might you have done differently? Discuss your answers with your instructor.

NH MA CT RI NJ DE MD NY PA VA NC SC GA

# ONLINE CONNECTION

Make a digital slideshow, video, or presentation about the powers of the state and federal governments that were included in the Articles of Confederation. Share what you've created with your instructor.

# WRITE

Do you think the division of power between the state and federal governments was fair? Why or why not?

...................................................

...................................................

...................................................

*Discover!* SOCIAL STUDIES • GRADE 4 • LESSON 20

# READ

## Problems With the Articles of Confederation

Imagine you go on vacation to another state with your family. You pass an ice cream shop and want to get some, but the shop cannot take your form of money. How will you pay for your ice cream? Having different forms of money made things difficult in the 13 colonies. The Articles of Confederation did not require states to use the same kind of money. Some chose to keep using England's form of money while some states created their own. This made it difficult for people to buy things when traveling through different states. It also made it difficult for states to buy things they needed from other states.

Since the federal government couldn't collect taxes, they had little money to pay for a military to protect the new country. They also couldn't raise money to make or buy things to improve the country. The federal government only had whatever money the states wanted to send them.

In future lessons, you'll learn a lot more about the United States' Constitution and the three branches of government it describes. These branches of government help the country run smoothly by sharing responsibilities. One branch makes laws, another approves and signs the laws, and the third decides if the laws are followed correctly. The Articles of Confederation only had one branch—the **legislative branch.** In this branch, Congress makes new laws. **Congress** is a group of representatives from different states that make decisions for the whole country. This was different from having to follow the rules of the king of England like the colonies had to do. The people could now have a say in how the country was run. Still, there were no other groups to make sure the laws were fair or that the laws would be followed in the states.

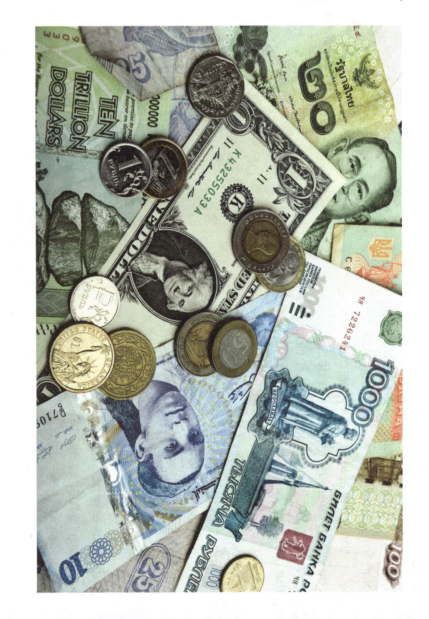

# PRACTICE

## Problems and Solutions

Think about the problems of the Articles of Confederation and the imbalance of power between the states and the federal government. How would you solve the problems? Write your ideas in the chart below.

| PROBLEM | SOLUTION |
|---|---|
| Every state had different forms of money. | |
| Congress had no power to tax the colonies and collect money for improving and defending the nation. | |
| The states had too much power and became like "mini-nations" that didn't work together. | |

# REVIEW

In this lesson, you learned:

- A confederation is a group of states that come together for a common cause.

- One goal of the Continental Congress was to write a set of rules called the Articles of Confederation, which would describe how the state and federal governments would work in the new country.

- The Articles of Confederation had many problems, including that it allowed states to have their own kinds of money and the federal government couldn't collect taxes.

**Think About It**

How do you think our government might look different today if we still had the Articles of Confederation?

# SHOW WHAT YOU KNOW

**Fill in the following sentences with the correct words.**

1. Leaders from each colony met in an important meeting to create a plan for the government of the new country. This group of leaders was called the _____ Congress.

2. "Colonies or states coming together for a common cause" describes a _____.

Select the correct phrase to complete the sentence.

3. The purpose of the Articles of Confederation was to _____.

   A. make the federal government more powerful than the state governments

   B. create a plan for the government that defined the powers of the federal and state governments

   C. give the state governments power to declare war

   D. establish a king of the country

**Circle the correct answers to the question.**

4. The Articles of Confederation didn't give the federal government enough power because the federal government could not _____.

   A. tax the states to get money to pay for a military or improvements in the country

   B. make treaties

   C. tell the states to use one type of money

   D. declare war

5. Describe at least two problems with the Articles of Confederation.

....................................................................

....................................................................

# PLAY

Pretend you were a representative at the Continental Congress. What argument would you make for disagreeing with the Articles of Confederation and creating a different document instead? Think of a few specific examples you might use to describe which problems are the biggest concerns to you. Then, act out a speech you might give to the Continental Congress to summarize your ideas.

# Lesson 21

## The Constitution

### By the end of this lesson, you will be able to:

- identify leaders who worked together to form the Constitution, including George Washington serving as chairman

- identify the importance of the Constitution in United States history

- describe a republic, including how much power is given to leaders and the involvement of citizens in choosing leaders

### Lesson Review

If you need to review the Articles of Confederation, please go to the lesson titled "Articles of Confederation."

### Academic Vocabulary

Read the following vocabulary words and definitions. Look through the lesson. Can you find each vocabulary word? Underline the vocabulary word in your lesson. Write the page number of where you found each word in the blanks.

- **chairman:** the leader of an organized group, like a committee (page ___)

- **citizen:** a person who belongs to a country and has rights and responsibilities within that country (page ___)

- **Constitutional Convention:** a meeting where delegates met to create the Constitution (page ___)

- **debt:** money that is owed (page ___)

- **delegate:** a person who represents their state (page ___)

- **draft:** the first version of a piece of writing (page ___)

- **Founding Fathers:** the writers of the Constitution (page ___)

- **republic:** a form of government that allows citizens to choose its leaders (page ___)

- **veto:** to stop laws or decisions from being passed (page ___)

## IN THE REAL WORLD

If you have ever written a long piece of writing, you know that the writing process has many steps. After brainstorming ideas, you write a draft, which is the first version of a piece of writing. Then, you revise it before publishing. Drafting the Constitution was challenging since many writers worked together and wanted their ideas included. They did not always agree on what to include.

When many people have different ideas, making decisions can be hard. Think about a time you got together with your friends and everyone had a different idea of what to do. How did you decide what to play so that everyone was happy?

# EXPLORE

The Articles of Confederation were the first version of a Constitution, but this set of rules did not evenly divide power between the state and federal governments. Colonists decided they needed something better. The men seen in the painting below gathered to sign one of the most important documents in history—the Constitution. It explains the rules and responsibilities of the federal and state governments and divides the powers in ways that make more sense for the United States.

Take a closer look at the image. What do you see? What do you think is happening? What do you wonder? Write some observations in the chart below.

*Scene at the Signing of the Constitution of the United States.jpg by Howard Chandler Christy is in the public domain.*

## IN THE REAL WORLD

When the Founding Fathers met at the Constitutional Convention to discuss the rules and laws for the United States, they had to fix the problems that existed with the Articles of Confederation. They knew each state had too much power and that the federal government needed to be stronger. The Constitution could make laws for the states to follow so that they would work better together.

Imagine if the kids in your family had all the power and your parents didn't have any rules. Maybe you wouldn't have a bedtime. Maybe you wouldn't brush your teeth every day. What could go wrong if you didn't do these things? What else could go wrong?

Create a list of existing rules in your home. Add a few new rules you would like to have. Share your rules with your family. Do they agree with all of the rules?

## I SEE...

## I THINK...

## I WONDER...

# READ

## Writers of the Constitution

Who actually wrote the Constitution? There were many people involved in coming up with ideas for the Constitution. The people that each state sent to help write the Constitution were called **delegates.** Let's read about some of the delegates and the different ideas they had.

George Mason.jpg by Boudet, Dominic W. is in the public domain.

Roger Sherman 1721-1793 by Ralph Earl. jpeg by Ralph Earl is in the public domain.

### GEORGE WASHINGTON

George Washington was the **chairman,** or leader, in organizing ideas that would be included in the Constitution. He wanted the Constitution to help the states work together better. He led many important conversations about the states coming together under a stronger federal government.

### JAMES MADISON

James Madison is known as the "Father of the Constitution." He had an important part in writing the draft of the Constitution. Madison believed the federal government should have more power than each of the 13 states. He wanted to split the national government into three branches (or groups) to balance that power. He wrote the Virginia Plan, which explained these ideas.

### GEORGE MASON

George Mason was a delegate from Virginia who was worried the federal government would have too much power. He did not want the Constitution to limit the rights of people. Some of Mason's ideas about people's rights and freedoms were included in the final draft of the US Constitution.

### ROGER SHERMAN

Roger Sherman also played an important role in drafting the Constitution. He was a delegate from a smaller state and thought that every state should have the same amount of people to represent them in future votes. Sherman feared smaller states might be ignored if they had a smaller population of people to represent them.

# READ

However, many delegates were concerned about the powers of people and leaders themselves. One delegate from Pennsylvania, Justice James Wilson, believed that people should be able to vote directly for their leaders. He also thought that the leader of the country should be allowed to **veto**, or stop laws or decisions from being passed without the approval of other branches of government.

*JusticeJamesWilson.jpg by unknown is in the public domain.*

## Importance of the Constitution

Although there were many different ideas shared, the writers had to combine ideas to come to an agreement that would work for the whole country.

The Constitution created the form of government we have and still use today! It gives us an outline for how the country should be run. It lists the rights of the **citizens**, or people, who belong to the country and have rights and responsibilities within that country. It points out basic rules for each branch of the government and gives citizens guaranteed rights and freedom.

# WRITE

If you had a chance to interview George Washington, what questions would you ask him about the process of writing the Constitution?

# ONLINE CONNECTION

Have you ever thought about what the Constitution looks like in real life? In 1787, important documents were written by hand rather than a computer. Today, we can see the Constitution on display in the National Archives Museum in Washington, DC. Ask your instructor to help you search online using the search terms "National Archives Museum + The Constitution." Take time exploring the document.

What do you notice about the way the document is written? What do you wonder?

# READ

## A Stronger Federal Government

The Constitution was a huge improvement from the Articles of Confederation in many ways. First, the government went from having one branch of government to having three branches of government that helped split up the power. The Constitution also allowed both state and the federal governments to collect taxes that helped the country pay off **debts**, or money owed, from the Revolutionary War. Another benefit was that the federal government would have the power to print money for the whole country.

While the Articles of Confederation gave more power to the states, the Constitution gave more power to the federal government. Can you see how the Constitution benefited the country more than the Articles of Confederation?

## Forming a Republic

The Constitution formed a new kind of government called a republic. A **republic** is a form of government that allows citizens to choose its leaders. The Constitution begins with the words "We the people." These words represent the importance of citizens' voices in making decisions in government. In a republic, citizens choose their leaders by voting. They have an active role in deciding how the government is run.

# PRACTICE

## What's the Big Idea?

By using the three pinned papers below, write an important fact or big idea about the Constitution. (You should write at least one fact or big idea on each pinned paper.)

Use your big ideas above to write a paragraph about why the Constitution is important.

..................................................................................

..................................................................................

..................................................................................

..................................................................................

..................................................................................

..................................................................................

..................................................................................

## REVIEW

In this lesson, you learned:

- George Washington was the chairman who kept everyone organized while writing the Constitution.

- James Madison, George Mason, Roger Sherman, and James Wilson shared their ideas about how the country should be run and helped write the Constitution.

- The Constitution formed a republic and explains what rights and freedoms citizens have.

- A republic is a form of government that lets citizens choose its leaders.

- Today, the Constitution still divides the power equally between state and federal governments.

### THINK ABOUT IT

The Constitution helped solve many problems in the Articles of Confederation. Can you think of any remaining problems to solve?

# SHOW WHAT YOU KNOW

Match each delegate of the Constitutional Convention to their description.

1. _____ George Washington

2. _____ James Madison

3. _____ George Mason

4. _____ James Wilson

**A.** wanted to divide the federal government into three branches; known as the "Father of the Constitution"

**B.** chairman of the Constitutional Convention

**C.** thought people should be able to vote directly for their leader; from Pennsylvania

**D.** did not want the federal government to have too much power; did not want people's rights limited

5. Circle all the statements that describe why the Constitution is important.

**A.** It gives all the power to the states.

**B.** It creates a plan for how the government should be run.

**C.** It guarantees citizens' rights and freedoms.

**D.** It was only written by George Washington, the first president.

**E.** It lists rules for the different branches or parts of government that are still used today.

6. What is a republic? How do the first words of the Constitution, "We the people," help describe a republic?

_____

_____

_____

_____

# PLAY

Pretend you are one of the delegates sharing your ideas about the Constitution. Talk about what you think is important to include in the Constitution. Ask a parent or sibling to pretend to be a delegate that has a different opinion about how power should be divided up in the Constitution. How will you come to an agreement?

# Lesson 22

## Slavery and Trade

**By the end of this lesson, you will be able to:**

- describe the role of slavery in America during the latter part of the 18th century
- explain the Great Compromise and how slaves would be counted as part of the population

### Academic Vocabulary

Read the following vocabulary words and definitions. Look through the lesson. Can you find each vocabulary word? Underline the vocabulary word in your lesson. Write the page number of where you found each word in the blanks.

- **abolition:** the act of ending or stopping a system, practice, or institution (page ___)

- **agrarian:** having to do with cultivating (tending to) land; agriculture (page ___)

- **chattel slavery:** a system of slavery in which the enslaved person is not considered a person with inalienable rights, but a thing that is possessed or owned (page ___)

- **Connecticut Compromise:** combined the Virginia and New Jersey plans for the legislature (this resulted in every state having two members in the Senate and each state having one member for every 40,000 residents in the House of Representatives) (page ___)

- **hereditary:** inherited from one's parents (page ___)

- **indentured servitude:** a system in which people perform forced, unpaid labor under contract for a specific period of time, often to pay a debt (page ___)

- **manumission:** release from slavery (page ___)

- **New Jersey Plan:** A plan for the legislature which would give each state an equal number of legislators (page ___)

### Petition Against Slavery

The 1688 Germantown Quaker Petition Against Slavery, written by Germantown founder Francis Daniel Pastorius, is the first protest against African American slavery in a public document.

The argument is based on the Golden Rule: "Do unto others as you would have them do unto you." It says that no matter what the background of a person is, they have certain rights that cannot be compromised. The petition called for the complete **abolition**—or ending—of slavery in the state of Pennsylvania.

Research this important document with your instructor and write one or two sentences describing what this document has in common with the Declaration of Independence.

- **transatlantic slave trade:** the European practice that started in the late 1400s to ship arms, textiles, and other goods to Africa; enslaved people to the Americas; and crops such as sugar, tobacco, cotton, and coffee back to Europe (page ___)

- **Virginia Plan:** a plan for the legislature which would base the number of legislators on each state's population (page ___)

# EXPLORE

If you never had to do any chores or work around the house, would you have time and energy to do other things? What would you do with that time?

This is one of the secondary ways enslavers benefitted from having an unpaid labor force. Owning and operating a farm or mill is difficult and requires long hours—but if you didn't have to pay people to do all that for you, it would be a lot easier to participate in other businesses, invest in other projects, or devote your energy to more creative pursuits, such as writing.

Think of our founding fathers, many of whom were enslavers. If they'd had to work their own farms and estates, would they have had as much time to publish essays and participate in political meetings?

Slavery was a huge part of the economy in America, and it had impacts that were obvious and less obvious. It can be very difficult to understand how slavery could happen alongside declarations that all men are created equal, and that the rights to life, liberty, and the pursuit of happiness are inalienable. The truth is, much of the freedom and prosperity some people experienced was made possible by the enslavement of others.

## IN THE REAL WORLD

There are so many wonderful modern conveniences and technological advances we enjoy today. You can order new socks with a few clicks online, and in as little as two days, a pair of socks made halfway across the planet arrives on your doorstep. But how much do we know about the process?

Most clothing will say on the tag where it was made. Research the conditions of the workers in these places to find out more about the people who make your things. If you research the country and brand, you can often find out more details about the workers who make your things.

Are they treated well? What is life like for them in their country? Discuss your findings with your instructor.

# READ

## Slavery and the Economy of the Americas

The **transatlantic slave trade** is the European practice started in the late 1400s to ship arms, textiles, and other goods to Africa; enslaved people to the Americas; and crops such as sugar, tobacco, cotton, and coffee back to Europe.

Remember the taxes that led to American independence in Chapter 2? Britain's colonial taxes around the world made up around 70 percent of its income at the time, and profits were large because of unpaid labor. So who profited, and how?

Slavery was involved in every part of colonial (and early American) economic activity, and every free person benefited from the practice.

- ship crews and port workers who transported enslaved Africans
- enslavers who profited from the sale of humans
- colonists who were able to produce, buy, and sell goods through unpaid labor
- British citizens and government profiteering from the global trade of taxed products produced by unpaid labor

These profits built estates, universities, historical buildings, banks and other financial institutions, and provided the investment funds for the Industrial Revolution.

The issue of American slavery is sometimes thought of as southern states having an **agrarian** (land-based, relating to agriculture) economy, which was supported by slavery, and northern states basing their economy on manufacturing and ending slavery earlier. This is oversimplified. The crops southern states raised were traded all across the United States, and northern states benefited just as much from having raw materials such as cotton, tobacco, and other goods at low cost.

## TAKE A CLOSER LOOK

### Traditions Today

Enslaved people showed much resilience throughout their oppression. One such ceremony, borrowed from British culture, recognized unofficial marriages by couples jumping over broomsticks. Enslaved people took up this practice, as they were not allowed to marry legally (it would have acknowledged that the couple had the right to enter into a legal contract, and enslaved people didn't have rights). Some African American couples carry on this tradition today!

# READ

## Slavery Redefined

Enslaved people were present in the New World before the British colonies, beginning in Spanish-occupied Florida in the early 1500s. Some Indigenous Nations practiced forms of slavery, usually by taking prisoners of war.

Historically, slavery had different forms. Anytime a person is forced to do labor without pay, it is a type of slavery. **Indentured servitude** required people to do forced labor as part of a contract, for a specified length of time. Sometimes it was due to unpaid debts or as punishment for a crime. **Chattel slavery** classified enslaved people as property. Enslaved people were not legally persons with rights, but things to be owned.

In 1662, a law in Virginia made it so the slave status of a child followed their mother. If a child's mother was enslaved, the child was born enslaved. This made slavery **hereditary,** or inherited from one's parents.

The South Carolina slave code in 1712 legally claimed that "Negroes" (a harmful term used to define Africans and other dark-skinned people enslaved in the state) were too "wild and savage" to be governed by the laws of the state, so they required different rules. The code became the model for other colonies.

Many people questioned how all men could have inalienable rights if some people could be legally owned. In attempting to justify this conflict, a system of laws defined certain men as having inalienable rights and certain people as "other" and "lesser," who didn't have rights. This created a new form of slavery: hereditary, race-based chattel slavery.

## TAKE A CLOSER LOOK

### Pennsylvania Abolition Society

American opposition to slavery is as old as American slavery.

Research the Pennsylvania Abolition Society and the New York Manumission Society (**manumission** means "release from slavery"). Find out when they began, what their purpose was, and who joined. Some of the members may surprise you—one was John Jay, the first Chief Justice of the Supreme Court. Alexander Hamilton and Benjamin Franklin were founding members of these groups too!

Discuss with your instructor how the views of these powerful people may have influenced state laws, then research the abolition of slavery in different states to follow up on your discussion.

# READ

## Who Is Being Counted, and Who Is Being Represented?

After the Revolutionary War, the United States had to set up how the government would operate. One major issue was how to set up the legislative branch, which writes the laws for the country. There were two plans that were favored: the **Virginia Plan**, which would base the number of legislators on each state's population, and the **New Jersey Plan**, which would give each state an equal number of legislators.

Large, populous states favored the Virginia Plan, because they would have more representation. Smaller states were afraid that their concerns would be overshadowed by states with more people.

There was disagreement over which plan to choose, but they settled on the **Connecticut Compromise** (also known as the Great Compromise), which combined both plans. In the Senate, every state would have two members. In the House of Representatives, each state would have one member for every 40,000 residents. Also, the House of Representatives would draft all laws that had to do with finance, the budget, and taxation.

Another problem arose when tallying the populations of each state to decide how many representatives in the House each state would get and how they would be taxed. Pro-slavery states wanted enslaved people to count for representation, but not taxes. States opposed to slavery wanted enslaved people to count for taxes, but not representation. To reach a compromise, it was decided that enslaved people would count as three-fifths of a person in the eyes of the government—but they were not given three-fifths of a vote.

## REVIEW

In this lesson, you learned:

- Enslavement was a major part of the American economy as a British colony and as a new nation.

- Even people who did not enslave others benefited from the practice, both economically and by living in a wealthy, growing society.

- Slavery in America was unique because it was written into law to be both hereditary and race-based.

- The Connecticut (Great) Compromise established two houses in the legislature, one with equal votes for the states (Senate), which was favored by small states, and one with votes based on population (House of Representatives), favored by large states. To appease slave states, enslaved people were counted as three-fifths of a person to increase their representation.

### Think About It

How do you think the growing disagreements between states regarding enslavement will affect the new government of the United States?

# SHOW WHAT YOU KNOW

Match the vocabulary term to its definition.

1. _____ abolition

2. _____ agrarian

3. _____ chattel slavery

4. _____ Connecticut Compromise

5. _____ hereditary

6. _____ indentured servitude

7. _____ manumission

8. _____ New Jersey Plan

9. _____ transatlantic slave trade

10. _____ Virginia Plan

**A.** a system in which people perform forced labor under contract for a specific period of time

**B.** release from slavery

**C.** combined the Virginia and New Jersey Plans for the legislature.

**D.** inherited from one's parents

**E.** a plan that based the number of legislators on each state's population

**F.** a system of slavery in which the enslaved person is legally considered property

**G.** shipped arms, textiles, and other goods to Africa; enslaved people to the Americas; and crops like sugar and tobacco back to Europe

**H.** the act of ending or stopping a system, practice, or institution

**I.** a plan for the legislature which would give each state an equal number of legislators

**J.** having to do with cultivating (tending to) land; agriculture

11. You may have thought and felt a lot during this lesson. Share your reactions, thoughts, and feelings to the information presented in this chapter. There are no right or wrong answers.

..............................................................................................

..............................................................................................

..............................................................................................

..............................................................................................

..............................................................................................

# Lesson 23

## The Importance of the Constitution

**By the end of this lesson, you will be able to:**

- describe the important ideas mentioned in the preamble to the Constitution
- identify the purposes of the Constitution

### Lesson Review

If you need to review the Constitution, please go to the lesson titled "The Constitution."

### Academic Vocabulary

Read the following vocabulary words and definitions. Look through the lesson. Can you find each vocabulary word? Underline the vocabulary word in your lesson. Write the page number of where you found each word in the blanks.

- **amendment:** an additional article added to the Constitution after it was completed and signed (page ___)
- **articles:** pieces of writing within a larger body of text (page ___)
- **checks and balances:** a system that ensures one branch of government does not become more powerful than the other (page ___)
- **framers:** the word we use for the people who wrote the Constitution (page ___)
- **ratifying:** to sign or certify something officially (page ___)

## CREATE

As you learn about the parts of the Constitution in this lesson, create a lift-the-flap graphic organizer so you have a helpful reference tool for this important document.

You'll need two sheets of paper. The first is a template with your flaps. It should look like this:

| Parts of the Constitution | |
| --- | --- |
| Preamble | Article 4 |
| Article 1 | Article 5 |
| Article 2 | Article 6 |
| Article 3 | Article 7 |

After you create your flap template, cut each flap where the dotted lines are shown.

Next, glue your flap template on top of the second page. The second page will provide space underneath each flap for you to write your summary of each section as you read.

# EXPLORE

Planning for the future can be a big challenge. You don't know what's going to happen! It's even harder when you need to make a plan that works for right now but will also work in the future.

Imagine planning a class. There are a lot of things to think about! For example:

- The purpose of the class and what students will learn
- What is expected of students and the teacher
- How students and the teacher will work together
- What the rules of the class will be

It would be a lot of work to plan all that out. Now imagine the class you design has to be taught hundreds of years into the future!

That's essentially the challenge the **framers** (authors) of the Constitution faced when making their plan for a brand new nation. They had no idea what the future would be like, but they had to plan for their current moment and ours—and everything in between.

What do you think they thought about when planning for the future? Do you think making those kinds of plans for the future can be done successfully?

## TAKE A CLOSER LOOK

### Who Were the Framers of the Constitution?

You might think of the Constitution as a blueprint for the nation. In that sense, the framers of that document were like architects. They had to decide what kind of legal foundation would be necessary to build the United States from the ground up, and what laws would enable the country to stand strong for hundreds of years.

But who were these architects? You'll probably recognize these names!

- John Adams
- Benjamin Franklin
- Alexander Hamilton
- John Jay
- Thomas Jefferson
- James Madison
- George Washington

# READ

## What Comes Next?

Once the Revolutionary War ended and the Treaty of Paris was signed, Patriots were left with an entirely new challenge: creating a new government from the ground up.

Democracy wasn't a new idea, but constructing a government of the people, by the people, and for the people certainly was! When it was signed, the Constitution was made up of a preamble and the main body, which contained seven articles. The purpose of this document is to provide the rules for the structure and operation of the United States government.

You might remember the term *preamble* from the Declaration of Independence. The preamble to the Constitution is not the law, but it introduces and explains the main intentions of the main body of the Constitution.

Here is the full text of the preamble:

"We the People of the United States, in order to form a more perfect union, establish justice, insure domestic tranquility, provide for the common defense, promote the general welfare, and secure the blessings of liberty to ourselves and our posterity, do ordain and establish this Constitution for the United States of America."

These 52 words explain the Constitution's six goals:

- form a new nation (union) that improves the ideals of governance
- create a system of justice
- preserve peace within the nation
- provide defense for the nation at home and abroad
- utilize federal spending for purposes of general national interest and benefit
- ensure that the promise of freedom is protected and lasting for future generations

## Think About It

The framers had to write a document that was broad enough to address issues that might come up in the future but also specific enough to apply in real-life situations. Are there any other major goals you would add to this list?

Share your thoughts with your instructor.

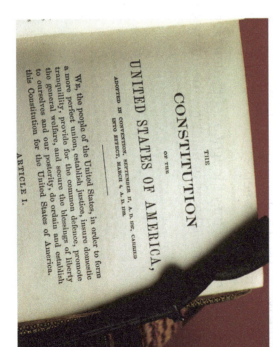

# READ

## The Seven Articles

The main body is made up of seven **articles,** which is a word that means pieces of writing within a larger body of text. These seven articles explain the structure of the government and how each branch, the states, and the entire federal government will work together within the law.

Article 1 is devoted to the legislative branch, Congress. Article 2 discusses the executive branch, which includes the offices of the president and vice president. This branch is responsible for how laws are put into practice, or carried out. The judicial branch is explained in Article 3, which is the federal court system. The Constitution also establishes a system of **checks and balances,** which are the limits on each branch's power and how it can "check" the other branches if they overstep those limitations.

Articles 4 through 7 deal with the roles of the state and federal government in making and enforcing laws.

Article 4 says that states can make their own laws, but they must also help enforce the laws of other states. Article 5 details the process for adding **amendments,** or extra articles, to the Constitution. Amendments have a different process to pass than regular laws, because amendments are much more powerful than regular laws. Article 6 says that the Constitution is the highest law in the United States, and that no other state or federal law can be written that goes against it. It also establishes that federal laws are higher than state and local laws. Article 7 establishes the process for **ratifying** the Constitution, which means to sign or certify something officially.

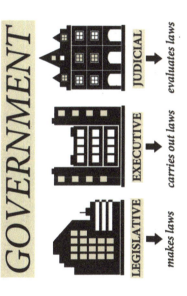

GOVERNMENT

LEGISLATIVE — makes laws

EXECUTIVE — carries out laws

JUDICIAL — evaluates laws

Memorize the preamble to the Constitution, put on your best colonial attire and recite the preamble for your instructor.

Here are some tips for a great recitation:

- Practice enough that you are very comfortable with the material.

- Use appropriate dramatic inflection to engage your audience.

- Make eye contact, smile when appropriate, and project confidence!

# READ

## Why Would We Need Amendments?

The framers of the Constitution needed laws that would establish a new nation as well as preserve freedom for generations to come. How can one document define what freedom means to hundreds of millions of people over hundreds of years?

The answer lies in the forward-thinking ideas presented in Article 5, which allows for amendments to be added to the Constitution. Since the Constitution is the highest law of the land, a law that gets added to it cannot be compromised by any other state or federal law. It becomes legally inalienable.

This is serious business! Amendments don't expire, and the only way one can be repealed is to ratify another amendment that eliminates it.

The framers couldn't have envisioned American life 100 years later, let alone life in the 21st century. Imagine George Washington seeing a space shuttle rocketing into orbit! But they did envision a future they couldn't predict and freedoms that had to stand the test of time. Our government is referred to as the "American Experiment" for a reason: No other country had been founded on the idealistic goals the framers presented.

### CONSIDER THIS

Often, some of our best ideas and solutions to problems come from our previous experiences. What experiences with the British government and life in the colonies shaped the Founding Fathers' vision for a new nation? How do you think life as British colonists influenced the laws they created?

Discuss your answers with your instructor.

# REVIEW

In this lesson, you learned:

- The Constitution is the document that established the United States government, and it is the supreme law of the land.

- It was originally made up of a preamble and main body.

- The preamble explains the six goals the Constitution will accomplish.

- The articles are the actual legal rules the federal government must follow.

### Think About It

Think back to what you learned about the Declaration of Independence. In it, the authors explained why the British government was no longer fulfilling its role toward the colonists. Does the Constitution solve the problems they identified? Why or why not?

# SHOW WHAT YOU KNOW

Read each sentence. Circle True or False.

1. True or False   The preamble is a set of laws.

2. True or False   The preamble explains the six goals the Constitution intends to accomplish.

3. True or False   The main body of the Constitution contains five articles.

4. True or False   The Constitution is the supreme law of the land for the United States.

5. True or False   The three branches of the federal government are Earth, Wind, and Fire.

6. True or False   The legislative branch can write laws that overrule the Constitution.

7. True or False   The legislative branch can amend the Constitution.

8. True or False   The judicial branch "checks" the other branches by determining if laws are constitutional.

9. True or False   The only way to repeal an amendment is through state laws.

10. True or False   The first goal of the Constitution is to form a more perfect union.

# CRETE

Imagine you're starting a new nation from scratch. You get to be in charge! What would life be like there if everything was just how you want it to be? What would it look and feel like?

Start by picking your nation's three most important values.

Next, write an explanation of each value—what it means to you and your nation. Use those explanations to draft your own constitution.

When you're ready, give your nation a name and present your new nation and its constitution to your instructor.

# Lesson 24

## Bill of Rights

**By the end of this lesson, you will be able to:**

- compare and contrast how Anti-Federalists and Federalists viewed the Constitution
- identify what additions Anti-Federalists wanted to make to the Constitution
- describe the Bill of Rights as a document that was added to the Constitution stating freedoms granted to people

### Lesson Review

If you need to review the contents of the Constitution, please go to the lesson titled "Constitution."

### Academic Vocabulary

Read the following vocabulary words and definitions. Look through the lesson. Can you find each vocabulary word? Underline the vocabulary word in your lesson. Write the page number of where you found each word in the blanks.

- **advocate:** to encourage support for someone or something (page ___)
- **civil:** legal matters that don't relate to criminal charges (page ___)
- **due process:** the steps the justice system has to follow to convict someone of a crime (page ___)
- **seizure:** when property is taken by the government (page ___)
- **self-incrimination:** admitting guilt or having to testify against yourself (page ___)

Non-profit organizations such as charities and private schools have founding documents that have a lot in common with our nation's founding documents. These are called Articles of Incorporation, which establish the existence of the organization, and bylaws, which are the structure, rules, and procedures the organization will follow.

When organizations want to make changes to how they do things, they amend their bylaws. Interview a local non-profit organization to find out more. Here are some questions you can ask:

- What is your organization's process for amending its bylaws?
- How long does the process usually take?
- When was the last time your organization amended its bylaws?

# EXPLORE

Have you ever had to negotiate the terms of an agreement?

Maybe you wanted to trade chores with a sibling, or agreed to play a game suggested by a friend, but you had conditions you wanted included in the deal before you would agree.

Think of that situation now and discuss it with your instructor. What happened, and how did you come to an agreement that respected your conditions?

When the Constitution was originally ratified, some people felt like they had conditions they wanted included in the deal. They felt that some amendments needed to be added immediately to guarantee that certain rights would always be protected in the United States.

Those amendments became known as the Bill of Rights.

## TAKE A CLOSER LOOK

### A Powerful Idea

The concept of a Bill of Rights is such an influential and powerful concept that many groups and organizations have drafted similarly modeled documents to **advocate**—or encourage support—for specific causes and groups of people.

- The National Youth Rights Association has written a Student Bill of Rights.

- Some states and cities have established legal protections for people who rent their homes that are often referred to as bills of rights.

- Nine states have enacted Bills of Rights for domestic workers, such as house cleaners, nannies, and home health nurses.

# READ

## A Difference of Opinions

In the six years between the end of the Revolutionary War and the Constitutional Convention, there was a lot of confusion between the states about how the country was going to operate. The delegates tasked with finding a solution at the Constitutional Convention quickly split into two factions: Federalists, who supported the Constitution, and Anti-Federalists, who thought the Constitution gave the federal government too much power.

It's not that the Federalists were opposed to individual liberties, they just felt that the Constitution said all that it needed to. They also felt like a strong central government, particularly the executive branch, was the right approach for the new government.

The Anti-Federalists were not quite as unified as the Federalists. Some were mostly concerned about states not having enough power. Some were mostly concerned that the Constitution did not do enough to protect the rights of individual citizens and wanted them clearly and legally guaranteed. Others complained that the Constitution set up a system that too closely resembled the British government they had spent years fighting to leave.

There are some notable names on both sides of the debate that you should recognize!

### FEDERALISTS

Alexander Hamilton

John Adams

John Jay

### ANTI-FEDERALISTS

Thomas Jefferson

Patrick Henry

Samuel Adams

## TAKE A CLOSER LOOK

### Which Side Is Washington On?

George Washington did not like the idea of political parties or factions. He understood that people often organize like-minded groups, but he felt that political parties tended to get too focused on increasing their power. He was also afraid of parties being motivated by revenge if they didn't get their way politically.

George Washington was committed to staying neutral and serving the nation with impartiality as much as possible.

# READ

## The Proposed Solution

Alexander Hamilton, John Jay, and James Madison wrote a series of essays and sent them to various newspapers to convince people to show support for the Constitution and encourage their state delegates to ratify the document. These essays became known as *The Federalist Papers*.

It took time to get the states on board, but the campaign was successful. Delaware was the first state to sign the Constitution, in December 1787. The final state to sign on was Vermont, in January 1791. Despite their eventual agreement, several states signed on after the Massachusetts delegation proposed a compromise: ratify the Constitution now and promise that the first order of new government business will be creating the Bill of Rights.

By the end of 1791, hundreds of proposed amendments had been whittled down to 12. They were approved by Congress, and the first 10 of them are what we now call the Bill of Rights.

# TAKE A CLOSER LOOK

### James Madison: Federalist or Anti-Federalist?

Though James Madison contributed to *The Federalist Papers*, you might remember that he was not on the list of notable Federalists. But he isn't on the list of Anti-Federalists either!

He was a strong supporter of the Constitution and aligned closely with the Federalists initially. In time, though, he decided the Bill of Rights was not only a good idea, but he was also the one to present the proposed amendments to Congress!

# WRITE

Compare and contrast the views of the Federalists and Anti-Federalists in the Venn diagram below:

FEDERALISTS

BOTH

ANTI-FEDERALISTS

Discover! SOCIAL STUDIES • GRADE 4 • LESSON 24

# READ

## The Bill of Rights

What rights did the Bill of Rights guarantee? Read on for a summary of the first 10 amendments to the Constitution.

1: Freedoms of speech, assembly, of and from religion

2: Right to own firearms

3: Freedom from having to provide lodging for the military

4: Freedom from unreasonable searches and **seizure** (the government taking property)

5: Right to **due process** (the justice system has to follow all steps correctly to convict a person of a crime) and freedom from **self-incrimination** (admitting guilt or having to testify against yourself)

6: Right to a speedy and fair trial, to face accusers, and to have a lawyer

7: Right to a jury trial in **civil** (non-criminal) court cases

8: Bans cruel and unusual punishment and excessively high fines or bail

9: Ensures that all rights not listed in the Constitution belong to the people

10: Limits the federal government's power to only what is written in the Constitution

# WRITE

Select one of the amendments in the Bill of Rights that means a lot to you. Explain why you think it is important and what you find most meaningful about it.

# REVIEW

In this lesson, you learned:

- At the Constitutional Convention, state delegates broke into two factions: Federalists, who favored a strong central government, and Anti-Federalists, who thought the Constitution gave the federal government too much power.

- Every state eventually ratified the Constitution, but only under the condition that amendments specifically protecting the rights of individual citizens be added.

- Twelve amendments were later presented to Congress, the first 10 of which are what we call the Bill of Rights.

## Think About It

America had just split from a ruling country that had exclusive power over the governance of the colonies. Anti-Federalists had several concerns about the nation's executive (President). How do you think their previous experience influenced those concerns?

# SHOW WHAT YOU KNOW

Write the correct amendment number next to each summary below from 1 (first) to 10 (last).

1. _____ Freedom from having to provide lodging for the military

2. _____ Right to a jury trial in civil court cases

3. _____ Bans cruel and unusual punishment and excessively high fines or bail

4. _____ Right to own firearms

5. _____ Right to a speedy and fair trial, to face accusers, and to have a lawyer

6. _____ Freedom from unreasonable searches and seizure

7. _____ Limits the federal government's power to only what is written in the Constitution

8. _____ Freedoms of speech, assembly, of and from religion

9. _____ Ensures that all rights not listed in the Constitution belong to the people

10. _____ Right to due process and freedom from self-incrimination

11. Now reorder the amendments according to your opinion of their value and importance, with 1 being the highest priority, and 10 being the least.

___ ___ ___ ___ ___ ___ ___ ___ ___ ___

PLAY.

Pretend you are one of the delegates to the Constitutional Convention, and you have a very strong opinion about whether or not your state should vote to ratify. Write a speech in favor of either Federalist or Anti-Federalist ideals and present your speech to your instructor. Imagine they are another delegate that you need to convince.

# Lesson 25

## Ratifying the Constitution

**By the end of this lesson, you will be able to:**

- summarize how the Constitution was adopted and ratified
- explain how leaders worked to educate people in their states about the Constitution so they would accept it
- describe more than one reason for the success of the Constitution

### Lesson Review

If you need to review what was in the Constitution, please go to the lesson titled "The Importance of the Constitution."

### Academic Vocabulary

Read the following vocabulary words and definitions. Look through the lesson. Can you find each vocabulary word? Underline the vocabulary word in your lesson. Write the page number of where you found each word in the blanks.

- **consent:** willing participation (page ___)
- **contradicts:** says something completely counter to something else (page ___)
- **Massachusetts Compromise:** Massachusetts agreed to ratify only if a Bill of Rights was added to the Constitution (page ___)
- **skeptical:** uncertain, doubtful (page ___)

### CREATE

Print and color pictures of these notable founding fathers/framers of the Constitution: James Madison, Alexander Hamilton, Benjamin Franklin, Thomas Jefferson, Patrick Henry, Samuel Adams, John Jay, George Washington, and John Adams. Glue each image to construction paper or cardstock to make them more sturdy and cut them out.

When they are complete, sort them into groups of Federalists and Anti-Federalists. Careful! A couple are a little tricky!

# EXPLORE

Have you ever been confused by something your parent or teacher has said because it **contradicts**—or completely counters—something they've said before?

Maybe you've been allowed to take certain toys outside to play or read independently at a certain time of day. For whatever reason, your parent or teacher may have done something different than you were expecting. Has that ever happened to you?

## TAKE A CLOSER LOOK

### What's the Expectation?

Think about a time you've felt similarly to the delegates at the Constitutional Convention that didn't like the rules being changed for the ratification process. Maybe it's one of the situations previously described, or maybe a friend tried to change the rules of a game when you were already playing.

How did it feel, what did you think about it, and how did you react?

It can be confusing and frustrating when you don't understand what to expect. This is how the Anti-Federalists felt about the process for ratifying the Constitution!

The ratification process for the Constitution was very different from the way things were ratified before, so some of the people who were **skeptical**—or unsure—of the Constitution felt frustrated by this.

# READ

## How the Constitution Came About

The Articles of Confederation provided a working agreement between the 13 original states for the early years of the new republic. But after 10 years, it was proving to be ineffective. In 1787, the Constitutional Convention was called with delegates from each state attending to discuss and debate what to do to improve the function of the new national government of the United States.

It was generally accepted that the Articles of Confederation had too many weaknesses. These weaknesses were:

- the growing national debt
- the inability of the federal government to collect taxes
- the lack of an executive branch to enforce federal laws
- the inability of the federal government to regulate foreign trade and trade between states

The Constitutional Convention originally set out to fix the Articles rather than replace them, but these weaknesses were too numerous to overcome with simple changes, and the states had gotten into the habit of outright ignoring any provisions they didn't like without consequence. Worse than that, under the Articles, the federal government had no ability to enforce the laws it did pass.

## Making Connections

Does this sound similar to the intent of another meeting between the states that had happened in the past?

The Continental Congress also had to pivot when reconciliation with Britain was no longer possible. One of Madison's arguments in defense of the Constitution was that it is a good thing for the government to change as needed when it is no longer working for the people, and the Articles of Confederation simply were not working.

## TAKE A CLOSER LOOK

### The First Civil War?

The Constitutional Convention requirement for a nine-state supermajority came primarily from wanting to avoid having to deal with one state in particular: Rhode Island.

Rhode Island had shown it was not afraid to be the lone state to veto proposals in the Confederation Congress. It was very opposed to strengthening the association between the former colonies under a more united federal government.

It wasn't until the newly formed government threatened to ban all trade with Rhode Island that the state agreed to sign.

Flag of Rhode Island

## How Would Changes Be Made?

The Articles of Confederation required changes to be "agreed to in a Congress of the United States, and be afterwards confirmed by the legislatures of every State." The Convention could propose a change to the Articles, but it then went to the states' legislatures for approval. Every single state had to agree for the change to be ratified.

The Constitution required only a nine-state majority to agree on the document in their state ratification conventions, bypassing the Continental Congress and states' legislatures entirely.

Federalists felt the Constitution was a document for the people, not the legislature. It should be decided by the people as a whole. The Articles of Confederation were being repeatedly violated, mostly due to states not agreeing to (or outright ignoring) the terms decided on in the Articles.

Anti-Federalists felt that the Constitution was already taking powers away from state legislatures, which shouldn't be done without **consent,** or willing participation. They saw the change in process as an overreach of power by the Constitutional Convention, since they were bypassing Congress altogether.

## Winning the Fight

Benjamin Franklin and George Washington were major supporters, but they weren't enough. A series of anonymous essays was published in various newspapers under the name "Publius" that eventually became known as *The Federalist Papers*. Alexander Hamilton, John Jay, and James Madison wrote these essays.

Several states agreed to ratify, but the growing concerns presented by Anti-Federalists began to influence state delegations. The **Massachusetts Compromise** came about when, in line with one of James Madison's ideas, Massachusetts agreed to ratify only if a Bill of Rights was added to the document. This compromise encouraged other states to agree under the same terms, and it was decided a Bill of Rights would be the new federal government's first task. The Constitution was officially ratified on June 21, 1788.

# ONLINE CONNECTION

Using online encyclopedias, research more about the Articles of Confederation. As you read, make a list of things the Articles of Confederation ensured Congress *could* do, as well as the things they could *not* do.

Make sure you have at least three entries for each.

When you have completed your research, share your work with your instructor.

**Drafting the Articles of Confederation**

York Town, Pennsylvania 1777 13c USA

# READ

## Strengths of the Constitution

Many good things about the Constitution make it an enduringly successful document:

- The system of checks and balances creates clear boundaries and more equally distributed power between the three branches of government, which prevents any one part of the federal government from becoming too powerful.

- The difficulty in amending the Constitution protects the document from political whims.

- The Bill of Rights protects what the United States considers to be fundamental basic rights that can never be violated by the government. These protections are what makes the United States a free country.

- The Constitution is the supreme law of the land, and no lesser law can contradict what is contained in the Constitution.

- This document affirms to the citizens of the United States and the rest of the world that a government can exist based entirely on the ideals of liberty and justice for all, even if the fulfillment of that promise has been a long and incomplete journey.

Arguments can also be made against the Constitution. Some argue the difficulty in amending the document keeps the government from responding swiftly to modern problems. The broad powers afforded to the executive have created a concern known as the "Imperial Presidency," a fear that in the modern era, the unclear language of the Constitution allows the presidency to grow unchecked.

# REVIEW

In this lesson, you learned:

- The Constitutional Convention required only 9 of 13 states to ratify the Constitution.

- Not all the states were on board; it took a guarantee that writing a Bill of Rights would be the new government's first order of business to convince enough states to sign.

- *The Federalist Papers* were an anonymously published series of essays written to convince the public to support the new Constitution.

- James Madison, a notable Federalist, encouraged the Massachusetts Compromise.

- The Constitution was a much stronger document than the Articles of Confederation, allowing the federal government to operate more functionally than before, when any one state could veto laws, and the government had no ability to enforce the laws that did pass.

## Think About It

Is it possible to create a perfect document to express the rights and responsibilities of a government to its citizens in a free country? Why or why not?

# SHOW WHAT YOU KNOW

Fill in the blanks in the sentences with one of the choices in the Word Bank below.

**Work Bank:**

| | | |
|---|---|---|
| unanimously | John Jay | nine |
| Publius | Bill of Rights | James Madison |
| George Washington | Massachusetts | Alexander Hamilton |
| Benjamin Franklin | Compromise | |

1. Under the Articles of Confederation, laws had to be passed _____.

2. In order to ratify the Constitution, _____ states had to sign.

3. *The Federalist Papers* were written under the name _____.

4. The authors of *The Federalist Papers* were actually _____ and _____.

5. National leaders _____ and _____ were big supporters of the Constitution.

6. In order to get enough states to sign for ratification, the Convention had to agree to the _____.

7. The agreement guaranteed a _____ would be added to the Constitution first thing.

---

## PLAY

Imagine you are responsible for convincing Rhode Island to join the other states in ratifying the Constitution. How would you convince them?

On a piece of paper, write a paragraph sharing what you think are the strengths of the Constitution and reasons they should ratify. Present your paragraph to your instructor.

8. List three strengths of the Constitution:

1. ................................................

2. ................................................

3. ................................................

# Chapter 3 Review

**By the end of this lesson, you will:**

- review the information from the lessons in Chapter 3, "The Constitution."

## Lesson Review

Throughout the chapter, we have learned the following big ideas:

- After independence from Britain, the Articles of Confederation was the first constitution of the United States, which was agreed on by the original 13 states to develop a new government system. (Lesson 20)

- The US Constitution is the most basic law of the United States. All other laws, including local, state, and federal laws, must agree with the US Constitution. (Lesson 21)

- The Great Compromise of 1787 created a two-house legislature: the Senate (upper house) and the House of Representatives (lower house). It also gave southern states the right to count slaves as three-fifths of a person to their populations. (Lesson 22)

- The US Constitution is a document established by the US government and is the supreme law of the land. It includes a preamble, which provides the rules for the structure and operation of the US government. (Lesson 23)

- At the Constitutional Convention, state delegates broke into two factions: Federalists, who favored a strong central government, and Anti-Federalists, who thought the Constitution gave the federal government too much power. (Lesson 24)

- The Constitution was a much stronger document than the Articles of Confederation, allowing the federal government to operate more functionally than before. (Lesson 25)

Go back and review the lessons as needed while you complete the activities.

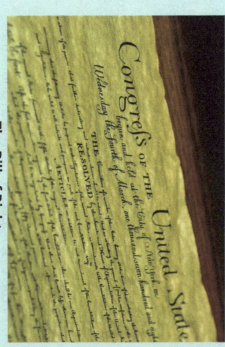

## ONLINE CONNECTION

### The Bill of Rights

The first 10 amendments to the US Constitution make up the Bill of Rights. James Madison, who was a Founding Father of the US government, wrote the 10 amendments to limit government power. He also wrote them to protect the freedom of citizens. Using an online search engine, research the first 10 amendments. Then, eliminate one of the amendments. Which one would you eliminate and why? Justify your answer by discussing it with your instructor.

# REVIEW

## Articles of Confederation and US Constitution

You learned that the Articles of Confederation was the first constitution of the United States, written in 1777. The articles were written by the representatives of the American colonies who made up the Second Continental Congress in 1775. When the colonies declared their independence from Great Britain in 1776, they realized they needed a new plan of government. The colonies deeply resented the laws that the British Parliament had imposed on them, so they set up a weak central government. The only branch of government was a congress with one house. Congress had power over military and foreign affairs but not over the affairs of each state. It could not enforce its powers or collect taxes.

Because of these problems, the states called a convention known as The Great Compromise of 1787, to write a new constitution. The new constitution strengthened the federal government and created the executive, judicial, and legislative branches, which had two houses known as the US Senate and US House of Representatives. Then, in 1789, the Articles were replaced by the United States Constitution, which became the supreme law of the land. The Constitution had six goals:

1. Form a new nation that improves the ideals of government

2. Create a system of justice

3. Preserve peace within the nation

4. Provide defense for the nation at home and abroad

5. Utilize federal spending for purposes of general national interest and benefit

6. Ensure that the promise of freedom is protected and lasting for future generations

### The Founding Fathers

Did you know that there were two Continental Congresses? In the first, Founding Fathers, such as George Washington, Benjamin Franklin, Thomas Jefferson, and Patrick Henry, met in response to the Intolerable Acts passed by the British Parliament in 1774. After the Boston Tea Party, the British enforced strict laws on American colonists.

In the Second Continental Congress of 1775, the Founding Fathers met to create the Articles of Confederation, which was the first step for the United States to declare its independence from Britain.

# REVIEW

## Federalists and Anti-Federalists

You also learned about the differences in opinion between the Federalists and Anti-Federalists on how to run a government. The Federalists included Alexander Hamilton and John Adams, who supported the Constitution. The Anti-Federalists featured Thomas Jefferson and Patrick Henry, who thought the Constitution gave the federal government too much power. The ideas of the Federalists soon became popular in essays compiled into *The Federalist Papers* and eventually led to the development of 10 proposed amendments, or the Bill of Rights, in 1791. The Bill of Rights is part of the Constitution. It gives US citizens basic rights, such as the freedom to speak and make decisions, to bear arms, and to prevent cruel and unusual punishments. The Constitution was also stronger than the Articles of Confederation because it created a system of checks and balances to prevent any branch of government from having too much power. This allowed the government to function more effectively because it ensured that no one was above the other.

Unfortunately, not everyone had the freedoms that were listed in the Constitution. Many of the Founding Fathers didn't allow enslaved people, who they saw as three-fifths of a person, basic rights. Slaves were often sold, beaten, and forced to work tirelessly in every part of American colonial life, such as farming and agriculture. These enslaved people, called chattels, could be owned permanently, including the children of slaves. It wasn't until the creation of the 13 Amendment during the Civil War in 1865 that slavery was abolished.

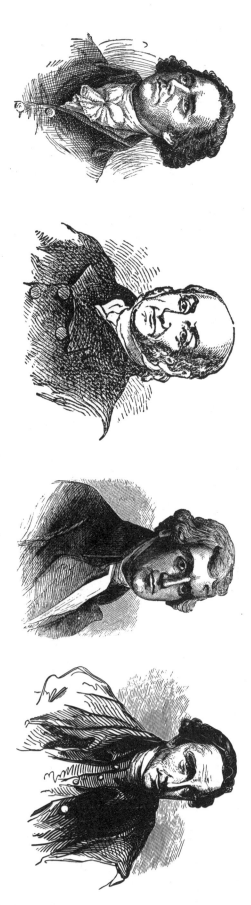

**Although these men had very differing opinions on how to run a government, they had to find ways to work together and create a government that they all could agree on. Even though it was difficult at times, these men were able to create a framework that our government follows to this day.**

# PRACTICE

## Visualizing Vocabulary

Let's review key words from this chapter. First, read each word and write its definition. Then, create a drawing that will help you remember the definitions

| Read | Write | Draw |
|------|-------|------|
| Articles of Confederation | | |
| Bill of Rights | | |
| checks and balances | | |
| Federalist Papers | | |
| Founding Fathers | | |
| ratify | | |
| US Constitution | | |

The words *amend* and *amendment* may sound similar, but they are used in different ways! The word *amend* is a verb to describe making small changes to improve something. If you accidentally broke your mom's favorite vase, you can make amends or amend the problem by buying her a new one. The word *amendment* is a noun and is used to describe a document that has undergone changes. For example, suppose lawmakers want to limit the number of trees that can be cut down. They can do this by proposing an amendment to make changes to an existing law.

# PRACTICE

## Venn Diagram

Compare and contrast the views of the Federalists and Anti-Federalists using the Venn diagram. You may refer back to the corresponding lesson or use an online search engine to help you complete the diagram.

**FEDERALISTS**

**BOTH**

**ANTI-FEDERALISTS**

## REVIEW

Did you notice that George Washington and James Madison, who were two of the Founding Fathers, are not listed as a Federalist or Anti-Federalist? While Washington supported the US Constitution, he felt that political parties tended to get too focused on increasing their power. Therefore, he was neutral and was neither a Federalist nor Anti-Federalist. James Madison, however, was a Federalist, but he also supported Anti-Federalist goals, such as individual rights. He did this by creating the Bill of Rights.

# PRACTICE

## Timeline

Use what you know about key events in American history to complete the timeline below. List the year, along with the features and accomplishments of each of the following events: Articles of Confederation, Bill of Rights, US Constitution, Great Compromise, Second Continental Congress.

| Event | | | | | |
|-------|--|--|--|--|--|
| Year | | | | | |
| Features and Accomplishments | | | | | |

## SHOW WHAT YOU KNOW

Think about what you've learned about in this chapter. Circle how you feel:

4 – I know this chapter really well. I could teach it to someone.

3 – I know this chapter pretty well.

2 – I am still learning this chapter. I am not sure about some things.

1 – I am confused. I have a lot of questions about what I've learned.

Talk to your instructor about your answers. When you're ready, ask your instructor for the Show What You Know activity for the chapter.

# Chapter 4

## Building a Democracy

Hi, friend! Monty the lion here, at your service!

When I got to the United States, I was very excited. We had landed in Boston Harbor.

Professor Tibbs told us the fantastic story of the Boston Tea Party. After seeing that and reading the Constitution, I realized how much the people of the United States value freedom.

Just as I thought this was going to be the best day of my life, something bad happened.

But don't worry. I roared through it!

When Maria and I went to get our bags, we couldn't find them anywhere. Someone had stolen them!

But then I saw a man with our bags. Maria ran after him because lady lions are faster than males. She caught him, but I came soon after.

I said to Professor Tibbs, "Where is the president? He needs to punish this crook!" The professor straightened his glasses and said, "That is not how it works here. First, you have to take him to the police, and then he will go to court. The president does not control the justice system."

I was amazed. In the savanna, the king judges everyone on their own. But Professor Tibbs said it is very important to separate justice from the government.

Turns out he was right, and I'm not lyin'!

## What Will I Learn?

This chapter focuses on the structure of US democracy. It analyzes the separation of powers and the reasons that structure was used.

## Lessons at a Glance

# Lesson 27

## Building a Democracy

**By the end of this lesson, you will be able to:**

- describe the process that was followed to choose the first president
- identify how long the president now remains in office
- describe reasons why George Washington is known as the father of our country
- describe the role important leaders played in our nation's founding

### Lesson Review

If you need to review how the US Constitution was adopted and ratified, please go to the lesson titled "Ratifying the Constitution."

### Academic Vocabulary

Read the following vocabulary words and definitions. Look through the lesson. Can you find each vocabulary word? Underline the vocabulary word in your lesson. Write the page number where you found each word in the blanks.

- **democracy:** a type of government ruled by the citizens (page ___)
- **elect:** to choose a leader from several options often by voting (page ___)
- **electors:** people who the right to vote in an election (page ___)
- **Electoral College:** the system that elects the US president (page ___)
- **Federalist Papers:** a series of 85 essays on the proposed new US Constitution and on the nature of government, published between 1787 and 1788 by Alexander Hamilton, James Madison, and John Jay to persuade New York state voters to support ratification (page ___)
- **popular vote:** the votes cast by the general public (page ___)
- **president:** the person who is the head of the government (page ___)
- **ratify:** officially signing, approving, or certifying something (page ___)
- **voting:** the process of a group of people making a decision (page ___)

**IN THE REAL WORLD**

You may have heard the word *democracy* before. A democracy is a type of government. Did you know that in a democracy the citizens hold the power? In the United States, when a person turns 18 years old, they can register to vote. They have a voice in who should represent a city, state, and country.

You have probably participated in some form of democracy. Have you ever voted with your friends about what game to play? That is a democratic decision. Voting allows everyone to have a say. Since democracy says majority rules, or the person or idea with the most vote wins, you will not always get your way. Democracy is a little different now, but the power remains with the people.

# EXPLORE

**The number of electors varies between states.**

What is the Electoral College? The US Congress established the Electoral College in 1789. The Founding Fathers did not like the idea of a popular election. They were concerned that **president**, or the leader of the US government, would always come from states with high populations. The Electoral College is not really a college as we use that word now. It is meant to mean a group of people with an unified purpose.

The **Electoral College** process is used to select the president and vice president of the United States. Each state has **electors**, or people who vote in the presidential election. The number of electors from each state is based on the state's representation in Congress. For example, the most populous state, California, has 55 electors. The least populous states—Alaska, Delaware, Montana, North Dakota, South Dakota, Vermont, and Wyoming—have three electors each.

The people in each state vote for the president. These results determine which electors are selected for that state. All the electoral votes for that state go for the candidate that gets the most votes in that state. However, two states, Maine and Nebraska, handle it differently. They award one elector to the popular vote winner in each congressional district. The winner of the statewide vote gets two additional electors.

**George Washington, the very first US president, was elected through the Electoral College.**

 WRITE

What is an elector? What is the number of electors for a state based on?

# READ

## The US Founding Fathers

The Founding Fathers helped the United States gain its independence. After the war, George Washington led the Constitutional Convention, where the US Constitution was created. He then became the first US president. In the United States, George Washington became known as "the Father of our Country".

Thomas Jefferson wrote the Declaration of Independence, and he was the third US president. He was also the first secretary of state. Jefferson's approach to foreign affairs as secretary of state was limited by Washington's preference for neutrality regarding the war between Britain and France. Jefferson favored closer ties to France, who supported the United States during the Revolutionary War. As president, Jefferson expanded the United States through the Louisiana Purchase from France. This land is now included in 15 US states.

Alexander Hamilton and James Madison, along with John Jay, wrote the **Federalist Papers**, a series of 85 essays about the US Constitution and **democracy** published in 1787 and 1788. The Federalist Papers led the states to support ratifying the Constitution. **Ratify** means to officially sign or certify something. The US Constitution needed 9 of 13 states to agree.

Benjamin Franklin secured French help for the war, which played a major role in the American winning the Revolution. He also helped draft the Declaration of Independence. He played a role in persuading the people to form a nation. He created the first US political cartoon. It was published in a newspaper on May 9, 1754, and it later became a symbol of colonial unity during the American Revolution.

James Monroe fought as a lieutenant and captain during the American Revolution. He later studied law under Thomas Jefferson. He became an ambassador to France. Later, he became the fifth US president.

**George Washington**

**Benjamin Franklin**

**James Madison**

**James Monroe**

**Thomas Jefferson**

**Alexander Hamilton**

# READ

## Becoming the First President

The United States votes to elect a president. George Washington, the first president, served two four-year terms from 1789 to 1797. Washington voluntarily retired from being president, establishing precedent for the two-term limit for presidents. Now, by law, a US president can only serve two four-year terms.

In the Electoral College, each state gets an elector for each member of Congress from that state. This process was created in 1788. In 1788, they had 69 electors. Due to expansion and population growth, there are now 538 electors!

**Popular vote**, the votes cast by the general public, does not directly determine the president. The popular vote determines the make up of the Electoral College. To win electors from a state, the candidate needs to win the popular vote in that state. The Founding Fathers did not want to use popular vote because they feared big states would hold too much power. They thought people would vote for candidates from their state.

During an election, each candidate has electors who will vote for them in the Electoral College. The candidate with the popular vote in a state wins that state. Their electors from that state then go to the Electoral College to vote.

## The Electoral Map

The United States still uses the Electoral College. Today, there are 538 electors. To win the majority, a presidential candidate needs 270 electors. California has the most electoral votes, with 55. Texas ranks second with 38 votes. Alaska, Delaware, Montana, North Dakota, South Dakota, Vermont, Washington, DC, and Wyoming have the minimum number of votes, which is three.

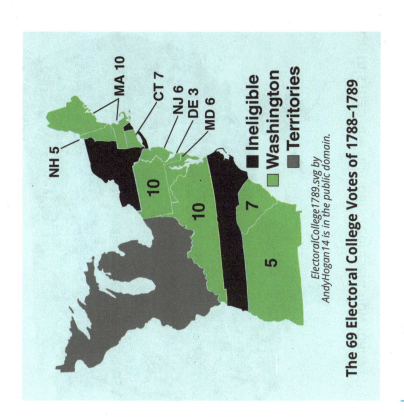

NH 5
MA 10
CT 7
NJ 6
DE 3
MD 6

10
10
7
5

■ Ineligible
■ Washington
■ Territories

*ElectoralCollege1789.svg by AndyHogan14 is in the public domain.*

**The 69 Electoral College Votes of 1788–1789**

 WRITE

How does a presidential candidate win the electors in the electoral college?

......................................

......................................

......................................

......................................

# PRACTICE

## REVIEW

In this lesson, you learned:

- America's Founding Fathers along with other influential citizens created the democracy of the United States.

- George Washington was the commander of the Continental Army. He also led the convention that created the Constitution and was the first US president.

- To become president, you must win the electoral college.

### Think About It
Why would joining a democracy be important to someone?

On this map, the numbers represent how many electors each state gets. Fill in the blanks in the paragraph below. In parentheses after each line is a hint or choice to help you.

California has _____ (number) electors, which is the most. Alaska, Delaware, Montana, North Dakota, South Dakota, Vermont, Washington, DC, and Wyoming have the least, with _____ (number) electors. Oregon has _____ (number) electors, and Florida has _____ (number) electors. To win the presidency, you need to win _____ (number) electors. The number of electors is based on the size of the state's _____ (choices: land/population). To win the state, you must have the _____ (choices: most/least) votes in the popular vote for that state.

# SHOW WHAT YOU KNOW

Circle the correct answer for each question.

1. True or False    People become US president based on the popular vote.

2. True or False    Benjamin Franklin secured French help for the American Revolution.

3. True or False    Thomas Jefferson was the third US president.

4. James Madison and _____ authored the Federalist Papers.

   A. James Monroe

   B. Benjamin Franklin

   C. Alexander Hamilton

   D. Thomas Jefferson

5. The US Founding Fathers created the _____ so that all the presidents would not be from big states.

   A. Electoral College

   B. Federalist Papers

   C. popular vote

   D. democracy

## PLAY.

Pretend you are in a debate about democracy. In this debate you are going to come up with points for democracy and then points against having a democracy.

• Discuss three points why a democracy is good.

• Discuss three points why a democracy is not good.

# Executive Branch

**By the end of this lesson, you will be able to:**

- identify the branches of government
- identify the leader of the executive branch of government
- describe the presidents cabinet and their responsibilities

## Lesson Review

If you need to review the US democracy, please go to the lesson titled "Building a Democracy."

## Academic Vocabulary

Read the following vocabulary words and definitions. Look through the lesson. Can you find each vocabulary word? Underline the vocabulary word in your lesson. Write the page number where you found each word in the blanks.

- **executive branch:** the government branch that includes the president and vice president that enforces the laws of the United States (page ___)

- **Founding Fathers:** the writers of the Constitution (page ___)

- **judicial branch:** the Supreme Court, which interprets and judges the laws (page ___)

- **laws:** a set of rules that the state makes people follow (page ___)

- **legislative branch:** the Congress, which makes the laws of the United States (page ___)

- **president:** the person who is the head of the government (page ___)

## IN THE REAL WORLD

### Rules

Who makes the rules you need to follow in your home? Think about one of the rules in your home. Do you think the rule is fair or unfair? Why? Would you like to be the only one in charge of how everything is done in your home? Write down your answers.

# EXPLORE

Do you know who the leader of your country is? Do you know who the people who help your country's leader are? Most countries have a leader, such as a president, prime minister, king, or queen. These leaders often have a cabinet, which is a group of people who help the leader run the country by providing advice and other forms of assistance. They help the leader to do their job more easily and effectively.

What if you became a leader all of a sudden? Pretend that you have your own country, what would you call it? Write down the name of your own country.

................................................................

................................................................

Are you going to be a king, queen, or president? Draw a picture of what you would look like as the leader of your country.

## IN THE REAL WORLD

### Being in Charge

Ask your parents or the person in charge of your home if you could be in charge of your house for one day or be in charge of a planned activity. What would you do if you were in charge? Would you make some new rules? If so, what kind of rules would you make? What kind of activity would you like to plan? What kinds of rules or directions would be useful for this activity?

Write down what happened and how you felt.

What are some **laws** you think your country needs? Write down at least three.

................................................................

................................................................

................................................................

# READ

## The Three Branches

After the United States declared their independence in 1776, the US government adopted the Articles of the Confederation. These Articles gave little power to the federal government. States were allowed to do what they wanted. They could make their own money. There was no national court system like the Supreme Court we have today. The states could not be taxed. The states began to struggle, and the federal government did not have a revenue source. The Articles of Confederation lasted until 1787 when the leaders knew that changes would need to be made.

The United States was a new country and needed a great leader to run it. During the Philadelphia Convention in May of 1787, the **Founding Fathers** of the United States came together and decided that the new government should have three branches: **legislative, executive,** and **judicial**. Each branch would have an important job. The branches would keep the others balanced so one branch would not become too powerful. It was decided that citizens would have representation through the three branches.

The chart below shows the three branches, who oversees the branch, and what their jobs are.

### LEGISLATIVE

- makes laws
- declares war
- oversees public money (taxes)
- approves treaties and presidential appointments
- conducts investigations and oversight within government

### EXECUTIVE

- signs and vetoes laws
- appoints judges
- proposes policies
- negotiates with other countries

### JUDICIAL

- examines laws
- overturns rulings of lower courts
- makes decisions but relies on executive and legislative branches to carry them out

# READ

## The Executive Branch

The US president is the head of the executive branch of government. The president gets help from the vice president, who is elected by the people, and by the cabinet. The cabinet is made up of 15 people. The cabinet is appointed by the president. They help and advise the president. The president, vice president, and cabinet all have different jobs.

Look at the chart below and read what each one does.

| PRESIDENT | VICE PRESIDENT | CABINET |
|---|---|---|
| ■ nominates Supreme Court justices and federal judges<br>■ has the power to pass or veto a bill that was passed by congress<br>■ submits a federal budget to congress<br>■ is the commander in chief of the military | ■ presides over the senate and casts the deciding vote if there is a tie<br>■ takes over the job of the president if they die or leave office | ■ in charge of federal departments, such as Education, Energy, Health and Human Services, and Defense<br>■ advises the president on matters that relate to or concern their individual departments |

## TAKE A CLOSER LOOK

### Secretary of Education

The Secretary of Education is a part of the Department of Education in the federal government. This person has several responsibilities. One responsibility is to determine the amount of money to provide for each state's education. They also will advise the president about educational matters. Above all, the Secretary of Education makes sure that the public schools are working effectively. The public schools make sure that the students are cared for and are studying the appropriate courses.

Why is the Secretary of Education's job important?

# WRITE

Write down who oversees education and why you think this is an important job.

.........................................................................................

.........................................................................................

# PRACTICE

The chart below lists each branch of the government. Use the Word Bank to write each job and group in the branch they belong in.

**Word Bank:**

| | | |
|---|---|---|
| vice president | cabinet members | |
| supreme court | makes laws | |
| congress | senate | |
| signs and vetoes laws | nominated by the president | |
| president | examines laws | |

| LEGISLATIVE | EXECUTIVE | JUDICIAL |
|---|---|---|
| | | |

## REVIEW

In this lesson, you learned:

- The US government is made up of three branches, which were created by the Founding Fathers.
- Each branch has a different job to help run the country.
- The Executive Branch is run by the president.
- The president can ask the vice president and cabinet for advice and to help run other federal departments.

### Think About It

Would the United States be a different place to live if the president made all of the decisions?

# SHOW WHAT YOU KNOW

Match the definition with the correct vocabulary word.

1. _____ president

2. _____ Founding Fathers

3. _____ laws

4. _____ legislative branch

5. _____ executive branch

6. _____ judicial branch

A. interprets and judges the laws

B. a set of rules that people are made to follow by the state

C. enforces the laws of the United States

D. the person who is the head of the government

E. makes the laws of the United States

F. the writers of the Constitution

# TAKE A CLOSER LOOK

## Important Moments in History

Pretend you are sitting in this room with the Founding Fathers while they are discussing how the new country's government should be run. Look at each person's face and the documents on the table. What are your thoughts about this important moment? Write them down or discuss your thoughts with someone.

# Legislative Branch

**By the end of this lesson, you will be able to:**

- identify the branches of government
- describe the role of Congress (Senate and House of Representatives) in making laws
- recognize the process a law goes through as it moves between the three branches of government

## Lesson Review

If you need to review the branches of government and the executive branch, please go to the lesson titled "Executive Branch."

.................................................................

.................................................................

## Academic Vocabulary

Read the following vocabulary words and definitions. Look through the lesson. Can you find each vocabulary word? Underline the vocabulary word in your lesson. Write the page number where you found each word in the blanks.

- **committee:** a small group of lawmakers who read, research, and debate bills before they are sent to the House or Senate for a vote (page ___)

- **House of Representatives:** one part of the legislative branch of our government; made up of a number of state-elected representatives (page ___)

- **laws:** a set of rules that the state makes people follow (page ___)

- **legislative branch:** the part of government that defines how Congress makes laws (page ___)

- **population:** the number of people living in a particular area, such as a state (page ___)

- **representative:** a person chosen to speak for others and to make decisions for the benefit of other people (page ___)

**IN THE REAL WORLD**

Everyone has rules they must follow. There are rules at home, at the store, even at the beach! At home, you might need to brush your teeth each morning and evening. If you want a candy bar from the store, you'll need to pay for it before you can take a bite. When you're at the beach, you must obey lifeguards and signs that tell visitors about safety precautions. What are some other rules you must follow, and how do you feel about these rules? Are there any rules that you would change? Why would you change them? What types of changes would you make?

- **Senate:** one part of the legislative branch of our government; made up of 2 senators from each state (page ___)

- **senators:** members of the Senate; each state elects two senators (page ___)

- **term:** the number of years an elected official holds office (page ___)

# EXPLORE

Have you ever played the game I Spy With My Little Eye? The rules of this game are:

1. One player tells the others the first letter of something they spy, or see, in their surroundings.

2. One of the other players tries to guess what was seen using this clue.

3. The other players take turns guessing.

4. The player that can guess correctly earns a point.

Play this game with a friend or family member. Then, try adding a new rule to the game! For example, "My new rule is that you may not spy anything that is the color blue!" How do the other players feel about the rule you created? What happens when you try to create a new rule together?

Now try to play the game without any rules! What happens? What does it feel like to play a game without any rules?

Throughout this unit, try changing the rules when playing other games you love! Do others agree with your changes? How do you handle having different opinions about the rules?

......................................................................

......................................................................

......................................................................

## TAKE A CLOSER LOOK

### Reasons for Rules

We may not agree with every rule, but it's important to remember that rules are made to help solve problems. Without any rules, people might not know how to act in certain situations. Look at the picture below. What rule does the sign remind people to follow? What problem does this rule try to solve or help people avoid?

# Legislative Branch

Just as you may disagree with your friends or family on the best rules for a game you like to play, citizens of the United States have different opinions about their country's rules. The **legislative branch**, also called the Congress of the United States, is the branch of government that makes the nation's rules, or **laws**. Each of the fifty states elects people they think will create the best laws.

The founders of the country, the men who wrote the Constitution, knew that creating laws would be tricky with so many states of different sizes. They decided Congress should have two parts. These two groups of lawmakers must agree, along with the President, if an idea is to become a law.

The first part of Congress is the **House of Representatives.** Each **representative** serves a two-year **term.** After their term, a representative can choose to run for re-election to see if citizens will choose to place them in Congress again. The number of representatives each state may elect is based on the state's **population.** The population is the number of people living in a place. The larger the state's population, the more representatives they may elect. California elects more than 54 representatives while smaller states such as Vermont and Delaware elect only three representatives each.

While states elect different numbers of representatives, every state elects the same number of **senators.** Senators are the members of the second part of Congress, the **Senate.** Each state elects two senators. This means there are far fewer senators than representatives. Senators are elected to serve in the legislative branch for six years. That's much longer than representatives serve.

Whether a lawmaker is a member of the House of Representatives or the Senate, their job is to solve problems in the United States. To do this, they think about new laws that might help citizens. When a representative or senator has an idea, they write it down. It's called a bill at this point; it's not a law yet. Before a bill can become a law, a majority of senators and representatives must agree on the idea. The bill is read, researched, and debated in a **committee,** or a small group of lawmakers. This committee sends the bill back to the House of Representatives or the Senate for a vote. Then the President must agree on the bill as well. The President's final approval and signature make a congressman's, or congresswoman's, bill a law.

# WRITE

What problems do you feel your lawmakers should help fix? What is an idea for a new law that could help solve one of these problems?

# READ

## Three Branches Make Laws

The executive branch, legislative branch, and judicial branch are the three branches of the United States' government. The writers of the constitution designed these branches to ensure that no one person, or one branch, holds too much power. They must all work together and cooperate to run the country.

Making new laws to help solve problems is an important job for the government. There are several ways a bill can become a law, but each branch of the government plays a part in making the laws. Look at the steps below to see how a bill becomes a law.

1. A senator, representative, or the President has an idea!

2. The idea is written into a bill and introduced in the Senate or House. (If the bill was written by a senator, it must be approved by the Senate first. If it was written by a representative, it must be approved by the House first.)

3. The bill is researched and debated in a committee, or small group of lawmakers. This committee will be composed of senators if the bill was introduced in the Senate and representatives if the bill was introduced in the House.

4. Once the committee approves the bill, the entire Senate or House of Representatives votes on the bill.

5. The bill is sent to a committee in the second part of the Congress to be researched and debated.

6. The second part of the Congress, either the Senate or House, then votes on the bill.

7. The bill is sent to the Executive branch, for the President to review.

8. The President signs the bill into law or vetoes the bill. If the President vetoes the bill, it is thrown out.

9. If two-thirds of Congress agree on the bill, they can override the President's veto, passing the bill into law without the President's approval!

You may be wondering how the judicial branch of the US government helps make laws. Well, the nine judges that sit on the highest court help decide whether laws that are already in effect are constitutional. If a citizen or the government feel a law is unfair, they can go to the Supreme Court and ask that they review the law. If The Supreme Court finds that the law is unfair, they can create a new law called a case law. The Supreme Court has the power to change our laws in this unique way.

# WRITE

Why do you think so many people must agree on a bill before it becomes a law?

...............................................................................................

...............................................................................................

# PRACTICE

Imagine you come up with an idea to solve a problem and you share it with one of your state senators. She loves your idea! What must happen for your idea to become a law? Complete the missing steps using complete sentences.

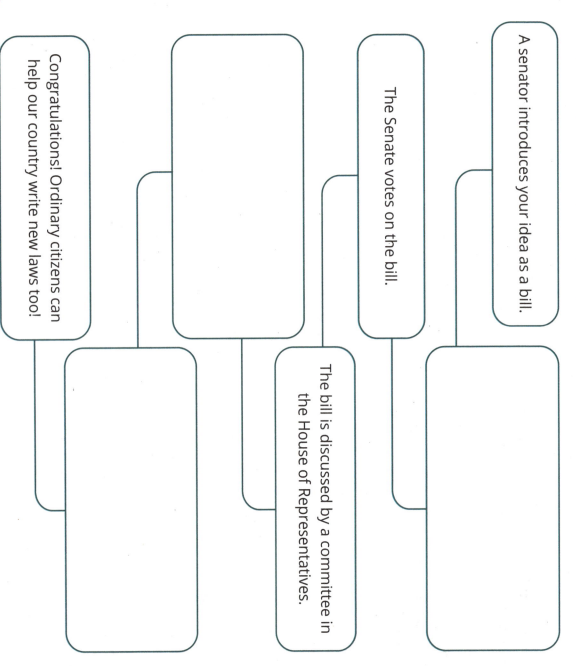

A senator introduces your idea as a bill.

The Senate votes on the bill.

The bill is discussed by a committee in the House of Representatives.

Congratulations! Ordinary citizens can help our country write new laws too!

# REVIEW

In this lesson, you learned:

- There are three branches of the US government: the executive branch, the legislative branch, and the judicial branch.

- The legislative branch creates new laws.

- Many people must agree upon a bill for it to become a law, including a majority of Congress and the President too.

- All branches of the government help decide which laws are fair.

## Think About It

Remember that laws can be challenged by citizens and members of government. The judicial branch, or Supreme Court, can change a law after it has already been passed. Why do you feel it is important for the Supreme Court to have this power?

# SHOW WHAT YOU KNOW

1. What important job does the legislative branch of government do?

..................................................................................................

..................................................................................................

2. What is an idea called before it becomes a law?

A. senator          C. capitol

B. representative   D. bill

3. True or False   The President must approve of an idea for it to become a law.

4. Order the statements from 1 (first) to 6 (last) to show how a law is made.

____ The President reads and signs the idea into law.

____ A senator writes and shares an idea for a law.

____ The potential law is sent to the House of Representatives.

____ A Senate committee researches and discusses the senator's idea.

____ The Senate votes on the idea.

____ The House of Representatives votes on the idea.

## TAKE A CLOSER LOOK

### Checks and Balances

The legislative branch must send bills to the President before they become laws, but senators and representatives can override the President's decision should he or she veto a bill. Two-thirds of both the Senate and House must agree on the bill in order to do this. Is this process fair? How could this power benefit the country? Share your thoughts with a family member or friend. Ask their opinion about this legislative power.

..................................................................................................

..................................................................................................

# Lesson 30

## Judicial Branch

**By the end of this lesson, you will be able to:**

- recall the branches of government
- describe the purpose of the judicial branch
- evaluate the importance of judicial review

### Lesson Review

If you need to review exploration, please go to the lesson titled "The Constitution."

............................................................

### Academic Vocabulary

Read the following vocabulary words and definitions. Look through the lesson. Can you find each vocabulary word? Underline the vocabulary word in your lesson. Write the page number of where you found each word in the blanks.

- **bill:** a draft of a law presented to a legislature for consideration (page ___)
- **checks and balances:** a system that ensures one branch of government does not become more powerful than the other (page ___)
- **government:** the making of laws and important decisions that control or affect all the people living in a community (page ___)
- **impeach:** to charge a government official with a crime (page ___)
- **Supreme Court:** the highest federal court in the judicial branch (page ___)

## TAKE A CLOSER LOOK

Did you know that Supreme Court judges are appointed for life? This means they cannot lose their jobs unless they are **impeached**, retire, or die. Supreme Court judges, or justices, must be nominated by the president. Being appointed for life prevents them from making decisions due to political pressure, like being persuaded to say yes or no to people in government. They do not have to worry about losing their jobs. Do you think it's fair for Supreme Court justices to serve for life? Why or why not? Write a paragraph explaining your answer.

# EXPLORE

Do you know the three branches of **government** in the United States? If you said the executive, legislative, and judicial, you are correct!

The executive branch includes the president, vice president, and the president's advisors, known as the Cabinet. The legislative branch includes Congress, which are people who create laws. Congress is made up of the US Senate and the US House of Representatives. The last branch of the United States government is the judicial branch, which includes the highest court, known as the Supreme Court. The judicial branch is also made up of judges and courts whose primary job is to make sure that laws are legal and follow the Constitution. You may recall that the Constitution is considered the "supreme law of the land" from a previous lesson. Take a look at this Supreme Court word collage. What do you think would happen to American society if the judicial branch didn't exist? Write your ideas on the lines below.

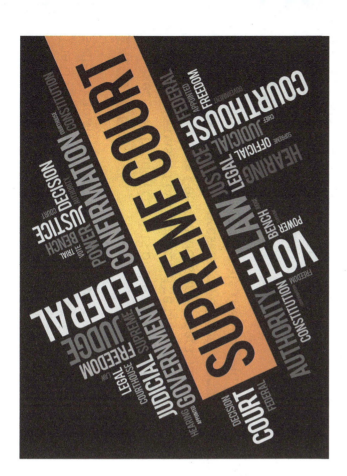

## Branches of Government

The US government has three branches. Each branch has specific duties to prevent any one branch from having too much power, a system known as **checks and balances.**

### EXECUTIVE

The executive branch consists of the president, vice president, and the Cabinet. The president can sign and enforce laws passed by Congress. The president can veto, or refuse, a bill before it becomes a law, and nominate Supreme Court justices and federal judges. If the president steps down or dies in office, the vice president takes over the presidency. Cabinet members are chosen by the president, and can advise the president on issues, such as climate change, war, education, and healthcare.

### LEGISLATIVE

The legislative branch includes Congress, which creates laws from drafts, called **bills.** Congress is made up of the Senate and the House of Representatives. If the president vetoes a bill, Congress can still turn the bill into a law if a two-thirds majority of the House and Senate agree on the bill. Congress can declare war and **impeach,** or charge, the president for any wrongdoing.

### JUDICIAL

The judicial branch includes the highest court, the **Supreme Court.** The judicial branch decides if laws are constitutional, or legal. The Supreme Court has nine members, called justices. Justices are chosen by the president and approved by the Senate. They serve until death, retirement, or their removal for any wrongdoing.

 EXECUTIVE

 LEGISLATIVE

 JUDICIAL

What are some of the duties of the executive, legislative, and judicial branches?

# READ

## Judicial Branch

The judicial branch determines whether or not a law is constitutional and does not break the rules of the Constitution. The judicial branch also has a hierarchy, or a level of organization, of federal courts. The lowest level includes 94 US District Courts, which cover different regions of the United States and handle most federal cases. Above this level are the 13 Courts of Appeals. At the top is the US Supreme Court, which is the highest court in the United States. The Supreme Court is made up of nine judges called justices, who are nominated by the president and confirmed by the Senate. Of the nine justices, there is one chief justice and eight associate justices.

## JUDICIAL REVIEW

Have you ever thought a rule was unfair, like choosing someone to be a class leader on popularity alone? Maybe you thought about making changes to the rule so it is fairer. The process of deciding whether a law is constitutional is known as **judicial review**. Supreme Court justices use judicial review to ensure that proposed bills follow the rules of the Constitution. If they don't, justices can send them back to Congress for revision. Justices may also amend a law. For example, a law may limit the number of trees that can be cut down in a certain area. However, these limitations may need to be revised if the original limits begin to harm the environment. Judicial review is a very important power, as the Supreme Court has the final say.

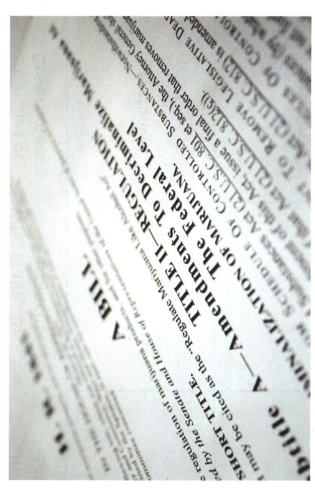

A US Bill

# WRITE

What is judicial review and why is it important?

.................................................

.................................................

.................................................

.................................................

# PRACTICE

| Branches of Government | Who Makes Up Each Branch? | Specific Roles or Duties |
|---|---|---|
| Executive | | |
| Legislative | | |
| Judicial | | |

## REVIEW

In this lesson, you learned:

· The branches of US government are the executive, legislative, and judicial.

· Checks and balances ensure that no one branch has too much power.

· The executive branch includes the president, vice president, and Cabinet.

· The president signs and enforces laws.

· The legislative branch includes Congress, which creates laws.

· The judicial branch has a hierarchy of courts. At the top is the US Supreme Court.

· The Supreme Court has nine justices.

· Judicial review is the process of deciding if a law is constitutional.

**Think About It**

How do checks and balances ensure that no one branch has too much power?

# SHOW WHAT YOU KNOW

Circle the correct answer.

1. Which branch in the US government is responsible for creating laws?

   A. executive      C. judicial

   B. legislative

2. Which branch in the US government is responsible for deciding if laws are constitutional?

   A. executive      C. judicial

   B. legislative

3. Which branch in the US government is responsible for signing and enforcing laws?

   A. executive      C. judicial

   B. legislative

4. What is judicial review?

   A. Congress comes together to discuss a bill.

   B. The president reviews a bill before deciding to sign or veto it.

   C. Justices decide whether a law is constitutional.

5. If judicial review did not exist, what could likely happen?

   A. The process of checks and balances would be disrupted.

   B. Laws could be passed that violate the Constitution.

   C. A and B

## ONLINE CONNECTION

Using an online search engine, research the system of checks and balances in the US government. Then create an infographic or poster to illustrate the main ideas of how each government branch does not become more powerful than the other.

6. Using an online search engine, research the story of Ruby Bridges, a famous child activist who fought against racism. Then, answer the following questions by writing a paragraph:

   - What issue did Ruby Bridges fight for as a child?

   - What important decision did the Supreme Court make in 1954?

   - How do you think this decision impacted society?

# Democracy

**By the end of this lesson, you will be able to:**

- identify how democratization has affected American life
- summarize how people are a part of the political process in the United States

## Academic Vocabulary

Read the following vocabulary words and definitions. Look through the lesson. Can you find each vocabulary word? Underline the vocabulary word in your lesson. Write the page number here you found each word in the blanks.

- **democracy:** a type of government ruled by the citizens (page ___)
- **referendum:** a special kind of voting, where people vote yes or no to making or changing a rule (page ___)
- **suffrage:** the right to vote (page ___)

### ONLINE CONNECTION

**Key Events Timeline**

Did you know that democracy was developed over two thousand years ago by the ancient Greeks? Using an online search engine, trace the history of democracy from the ancient Greeks to present-day society by creating a timeline. In your timeline, include key events, such as the United States Constitution, that helped create a democratic government.

**The United States Constitution**

# EXPLORE

Do you know what the word *democracy* means? **Democracy** comes from two Greek words, *demos* and *kratos*, that mean "rule by the people." In democracy, people have a say in simple things, such as coming up with a name for a class pet, or complicated issues, such as how the government is run. People usually do this by making a decision through *voting*. If you have ever voted on a name for a class pet or who you think the next class president should be, then you have experienced the democratic process! Take a look at the image below showing students voting in class by raising their hands. Why do you think voting is important? How do you think it affects people in society? Write your ideas in the lines to the right.

**Students voting in a class.**

# READ

## Origins and Effects of Democracy

The first civilization to develop a democracy was ancient Greece. All citizens came together to form an assembly. They talked about the kinds of laws they wanted by placing pebbles in urns to vote. By the 1600s, early American colonists began to think that all people had certain rights, such as the right to participate in their government. This led to the establishment of democracy in the US and changed American life. Today, people have the freedom to speak and make important decisions, such as who can vote. This is called **suffrage**, or the right to vote, and is given to US citizens who are at least 18 years of age. Prisoners do not have the right to vote.

Democracy has also affected American life by placing limitations on the time a person can serve in the government. For example, presidents can only serve two terms. After a term, or four years, presidents are reelected or replaced by another person. This gives citizens a chance to select a new president if they disagree with their beliefs or ideas. The number of people who vote also matters. Many decisions in society are determined by whether citizens understand or agree on an issue. For example, if people do not understand that climate change can be caused by burning fossil fuels, they may be less likely to vote on laws to protect the environment.

**Pebbles were used to vote in ancient Greece.**

## WRITE

How can democracy affect American life?

........................................................................

........................................................................

........................................................................

........................................................................

........................................................................

........................................................................

........................................................................

........................................................................

## READ

### Forms of Democracy

Did you know there are two forms of democracy in the United States? In a *direct democracy*, all the voters come together in one place to make decisions and laws. This can be done through a special kind of voting called a **referendum**, where people vote *yes* or *no* to making or changing a rule. If your teacher asked the class to vote on changing taco Tuesdays to tamale Tuesdays and the class voted *no*, your teacher gave you a referendum! Direct democracies are usually effective in small communities because there are fewer people. Citizens can express their opinions and beliefs and make decisions by voting. However, direct democracies are not effective to run a country because it is hard to assemble millions of people to make decisions and laws.

To solve the problem of *direct democracies*, people elect *representatives*, or people in the government, to speak for them. This form of democracy is called an *indirect democracy* because decisions and laws are not directly created by citizens. Instead citizens speak to elected representatives who help make decisions and laws for society. This is important because it ensures citizens the freedom to speak and make decisions, which are important principles of democracy. Citizens also have the right to free and fair elections.

**US Voting Booth**

## WRITE

How do people play a role in direct and indirect democracies?

........................................................

........................................................

........................................................

........................................................

........................................................

# PRACTICE

Use what you know about democracy to complete the table below.

| Forms of Democracy | Features | How American Life Is Affected |
|---|---|---|
| Direct | | |
| Indirect | | |

# REVIEW

In this lesson, you learned:

- The first civilization to develop a democracy was ancient Greece.
- Democracy gives citizens the freedom to speak, make decisions, and the right to free and fair elections.
- Democracy places limitations on the time a person can serve in the US government.
- The two forms of democracy in the US are direct and indirect.
- In a direct democracy, all voters come together to make decisions and laws.
- Direct democracies use a special kind of voting called a referendum.
- In an indirect democracy, people elect representatives.

**Think About It**
What are some of the problems with democracy?

# SHOW WHAT YOU KNOW

Circle the correct answers for each question.

**1.** What is one way that democracy has affected American life? Circle all correct answers.

**A.** Presidents can only serve two terms, giving citizens a chance to reelect or replace a president.

**B.** If people do not understand or agree on an issue, they may be less likely to vote on laws.

**C.** People have become friendlier to each other, because citizens have the freedom to speak.

**2.** How do people participate in a direct democracy?

**A.** People elect representatives who help make decisions and laws in society.

**B.** People use a referendum to vote yes or no on an issue.

**C.** Both A and B.

**3.** How do people participate in an indirect democracy?

**A.** People elect representatives to speak for them.

**B.** All the voters come together in one place to make decisions and laws.

**C.** Both A and B

## ONLINE CONNECTION

### Democratic Government

Did you know that the United States is one of several countries in the world that has a democratic government? Using an online search engine, research other countries that have democracies. Investigate the different types of democracies that exist or the titles of elected officials. How are they similar or different to the democracy in the United States? Share your findings by discussing them with your instructor.

**4.** What is a referendum? How does a referendum affect American life?

...................................................................................................

...................................................................................................

...................................................................................................

## Chapter 4 Review

**By the end of this lesson, you will:**

- review the information from the lessons in Chapter 4, "Building a Democracy."

### Lesson Review

Throughout the chapter, we have learned the following big ideas:

- To become president of the United States, a person must win the Electoral College, which is a system of officials that chooses the president, such as George Washington. (Lesson 27)

- The executive, legislative, and judicial branches make up the three branches of the United States government. The executive branch is responsible for signing and enforcing laws. (Lesson 28)

- The legislative branch creates new laws from bills. Bills must be approved by Congress and the president of the United States before they become laws. (Lesson 29)

- The judicial branch interprets and decides if laws are constitutional or legal. The judicial branch includes federal judges and US Supreme Court justices. (Lesson 30)

- Democracy gives citizens the freedom to speak and make decisions. They also give people the right to have free and fair elections. (Lesson 31)

Go back and review the lessons as needed while you complete the activities.

## IN THE REAL WORLD

Have you ever wanted to write a letter to a government leader? What important issue would you like the leader to address? Research a topic or issue that you are interested in, such as climate change, animal conservation, or healthcare. Then, write a letter to a leader to discuss your concerns and ideas for a better society and future. If you need help writing a letter, discuss your ideas with your instructor. You can also look for articles online on how to write a formal letter. Then have your instructor help you mail the letter to the government leader.

# REVIEW

## Branches of Government

In this chapter, we learned about the three branches of government in the United States. They include the executive, legislative, and judicial branches, with each having specific roles and duties. The executive branch consists of the president, vice president, and the cabinet. In the executive branch, the president has the power to sign and enforce laws. The legislative branch includes Congress, which are people who create laws. Congress is made up of the US Senate and the US House of Representatives. Congress can also declare war and impeach the president of any wrongdoing. The last branch of the United States government is the judicial branch, which includes the Supreme Court. The judicial branch decides if laws are legal.

## How a Bill Becomes a Law

We also learned the process of how a bill becomes a law:

1. A bill comes from ideas proposed by citizens like you!

2. The bill goes to a special committee of experts, which reviews the bill. When the bill reaches the House, representatives take a vote. If two-thirds of the representatives agree on the bill, it goes to the Senate.

3. Once the bill reaches the Senate, senators will discuss and vote. If two-thirds of senators agree on the bill, it goes to the president for review.

4. When the bill reaches the president, they can sign and pass it. If this happens, the bill becomes a law. The president can also veto the bill. If this happens, the bill can still become a law if two-thirds of both the House and Senate agree on the bill.

TAKE A CLOSER LOOK

The three branches of government work in Washington, D.C., the capitol of the United States. This image shows the Capitol Building, where the US House of Representatives and US Senate meet to discuss and vote on new laws. Senators and representatives each have an office where they conduct research and hold meetings. There are also large meeting rooms called galleries where the entire Congress can sit together to discuss the country's needs.

**The US Capitol**

# REVIEW

## The Electoral College and Effects of Democracy

Recall that the Electoral College was established by the Founding Fathers in 1789. The Founding Fathers did not want a popular election, or votes directly from citizens. They were concerned that presidents could come from states with high populations. They also worried that citizens did not have the knowledge to make the right choice. To solve this, they created a way for citizens to vote and select electors. Electors from each state then vote for the president. Whoever gets the most electors wins the presidency.

We have also learned about how democracy affects American life. There are two forms of democracy in the United States: direct democracy and indirect democracy. A direct democracy means all voters come together in one place to make decisions and laws. This can be done through a special kind of voting called a referendum, where people vote yes or no to making or changing a rule. Citizens can also express their opinions and beliefs and make decisions by voting. However, direct democracies are not effective to run a country because it is hard to assemble millions of people to make decisions and laws.

An indirect democracy means people elect representatives, or people in the government, to speak for them. Citizens do not directly make decisions and laws; rather, they speak to elected representatives to do this for them. This is important because it ensures citizens the freedom to speak and make decisions, which are important principles of democracy. Citizens also have the right to free and fair elections.

### Electoral votes (electors) per state

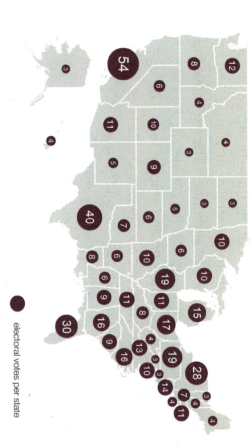

● electoral votes per state

## WRITE

What kind of democracy does the United States have? Why did the Founding Fathers choose to use an electoral college rather than having the people vote themselves?

# PRACTICE

## Visualizing Vocabulary

Write a brief definition or description of each vocabulary word in the space titled "Write." On a blank piece of paper, draw a picture of two or three vocabulary words to help you remember their meanings.

 REVIEW

Did you know that the word *bill* can have two different meanings? In government, a bill is a draft of a law presented to a legislature for consideration. However, a bill can also mean a unit of currency, like a dollar bill! To avoid confusion, people can differentiate the two by saying legislative bill (a draft of a law) or dollar bill (money).

**One US dollar bill**

| Read | Write |
|------|-------|
| electoral college | |
| executive branch | |
| legislative branch | |
| judicial branch | |
| bill | |
| laws | |
| congress | |
| democracy | |
| referendum | |

# PRACTICE

## Bubble Map

Bubble maps are used to organize information. Use what you know about the branches of government in the United States to complete the bubble chart. Start from the center of the circle and work your way out. Then for each branch of government, write down its features by filling in the smaller circles. You may refer back to the worktext as needed.

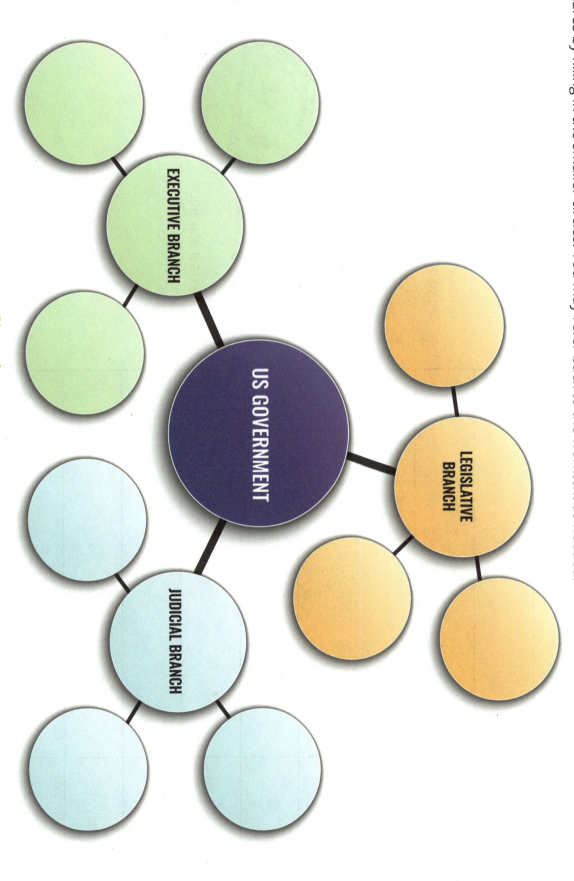

EXECUTIVE BRANCH

US GOVERNMENT

LEGISLATIVE BRANCH

JUDICIAL BRANCH

# PRACTICE

## Forms of Democracy

Use what you know about democracy to complete the table below.

| Forms of Democracy | Features | How American Life Is Affected |
|---|---|---|
| Direct | | |
| Indirect | | |

## SHOW WHAT YOU KNOW

Think about what you have learned about in this chapter. Circle how you feel:

4 – I know this chapter really well. I could teach it to someone.

3 – I know this chapter pretty well.

2 – I am still learning this chapter. I am not sure about some things.

1 – I am confused. I have a lot of questions about what I have learned.

Talk to your instructor about your answers. When you are ready, ask your instructor for the Show What You Know activity for the chapter.

# Chapter 5

## Explorations West

Hi! Monty the lion again!

I am visiting the United States. Everything is so different here!

Last time, my wife Maria caught a thief trying to steal our luggage! We took him to the police. They arrested him, and he was given a fair trial. The judges and jury looked carefully at the facts and put him in jail.

That was just the start of everything we were going to learn about this country. So, let's roar through this!

The trial was over. I asked Professor Tibbs if this courthouse is where every US citizen was judged. He laughed and said, "This country is huge, and there are courts and judges all over!"

He showed me a map of how big the country is. I was amazed and asked, "How did the country get so big?"

Professor Tibbs explained that, at first, the United States had only 13 states. Many people moved here. They began traveling west and creating more states until they reached the 50 that exist today.

Maria asked, "Was the west empty?" Professor Tibbs said, "No, Native Americans lived in all the states. Some of the areas belonged to other countries like Spain and France."

Professor Tibbs said, "That is quite a story." I love a good story. I wanted to go west and see all the places those explorers found!

We have a lot of adventures ahead of us, and I'm not lyin'!

## What Will I Learn?

This chapter examines the westward expansion of the United States in the late eighteenth and nineteenth centuries.

## Lessons at a Glance

# The Northwest Territory

**By the end of this lesson, you will be able to:**

- identify how the land in the Northwest Territory was organized and divided

- describe the rules that were established in the Northwest Ordinance and their effect on the Americans and the Indigenous people

- describe how the expansion into the Northwest Territory created conflict between Americans and Indigenous people and the effects of these conflicts

## Lesson Review

If you need to review westward expansion, please go to the lesson titled "Results of the French and Indian War."

## Academic Vocabulary

Read the following vocabulary words and definitions. Look through the lesson. Can you find each vocabulary word? Underline the vocabulary word in your lesson. Write the page number of where you found each word in the blanks.

- **alliance:** an agreement between two groups to help each other (page ____)

- **conflict:** fighting/arguing that happens when people strongly disagree (page ____)

- **ordinances:** laws (page ____)

- **territory:** land that is run by a government but is not yet a state (page ____)

# CREATE

As you learn about history, it is important to understand the order in which things happened to help you understand the different events. One event can sometimes lead to or trigger another event. This is often the case when people were exploring new land. As you work through the lesson, pay attention to the dates of important events. As you read, create a timeline of the important events to help you organize and understand what took place.

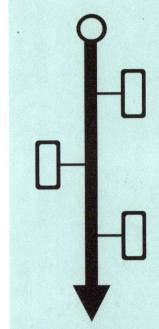

# EXPLORE

Many of the settlers that moved to the Northwest Territory must have been wondering the same things as you! Read to find out more about the Northwest Territory and how the United States continued to expand. As you read, think about the questions that you asked yourself. Do you think the settlers felt the same way as you? Did any of your answers change as you learned more?

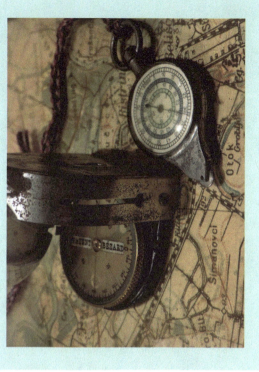

Imagine that you and your family have been given the opportunity to move to a new area that has never been explored before. What an adventure! You will pack up your belongings and begin your journey to this new area with a few other families.

Draw a picture of what you imagine your journey might look like. Then, answer the questions about your journey.

How are you feeling? ...............................................................................

What are you most excited about? .........................................................

What are you most nervous about? .........................................................

What are you wondering about? ..............................................................

What will you need to do first once you arrive? ....................................

# READ

## Expansion Into the Northwest Territory

At the end of the French and Indian War in 1763, the United States took control of the Northwest Territory. A **territory** is land that is run by a government but is not yet a state. The Northwest Territory was land that had never been explored by settlers before. Can you imagine what it would be like to live there?

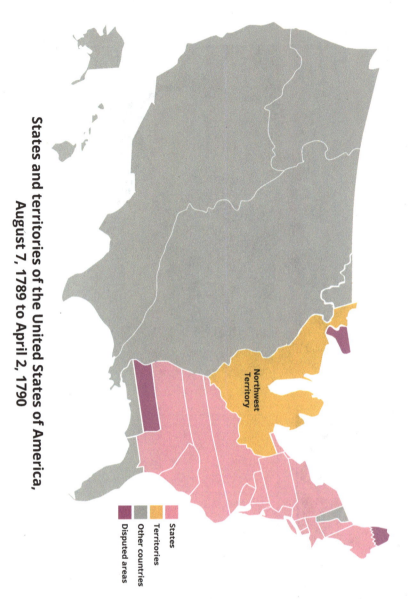

**States and territories of the United States of America, August 7, 1789 to April 2, 1790**

Northwest Territory

- Disputed areas
- Other countries
- Territories
- States

The Land Ordinance also explained how each town would be organized. Each township would have 36 lots, or pieces of land. One lot was set aside for a public school, four lots were given to veterans, and the rest of the lots were sold to the public. Imagine you were given new land and you had to divide it up. What would you do with each lot? Write your ideas on the lines below.

## The Land Ordinance of 1785

What do you think was one of the first things settlers needed to do with the new territory? They needed to divide up the land. Congress created **ordinances**, or laws, that explained how the land would be split.

# READ

## The Northwest Ordinance of 1787

You might be wondering if there would be any rules or laws in this new territory. Have you ever heard of the Northwest Ordinance of 1787? The Northwest Ordinance of 1787 created laws for the territory.

- Public education must be provided.
- Slavery was not allowed.
- People could practice their own religion.
- No land would be taken from the Indigenous people.

The Northwest Ordinance of 1787 also explained how the lands could become states. The territory would have to:

- reach a population of 60,000 free people
- write a constitution
- ask Congress to become a state

What an exciting time for the settlers! This meant that there could be new states added to the United States. However, this meant that settlers would be traveling to and living in areas where the Indigenous people already lived. Can you imagine what it would be like to be one of the first people to live in a brand new state?

## ONLINE CONNECTION

### Northwest Territory (1787)

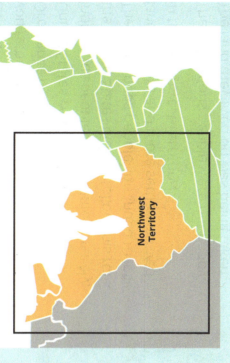

Northwest Territory

| | |
|---|---|
| Ohio, 1803 | Michigan, 1837 |
| Indiana, 1816 | Wisconsin, 1848 |
| Illinois, 1818 | Minnesota, 1858 |

This map shows the land that the Northwest Territory covered. You can also see the states that were created and what year each of them became a state. Why might they have become states in the order that they did?

## WRITE

Think about the rules in the Northwest Ordinance of 1787. Do you think everyone followed the rules? Do you think everyone agreed with these rules? Why or why not?

........................................................................

........................................................................

........................................................................

# READ

## Conflict in The Northwest Territory

When two people or groups of people want the same thing, what usually happens? There is often conflict. **Conflict** is when people strongly disagree about something. This is what happened in the Northwest Territory. Do you remember the rule in the Northwest Ordinance of 1787? It stated that the United States would never take the Indigenous people's land. Unfortunately, the United States did not follow this rule. The Indigenous people continued to lose land as more and more settlers arrived in the Northwest Territory.

The Indigenous people were not happy. The land they lived on was being taken away! In order to protect their land, they formed an alliance with other Indigenous people. An **alliance** is an agreement made between two or more people or groups of people. The alliance fought against the settlers and the American army.

After years of fighting, the Indigenous people signed an agreement with the United States in 1795. Even with the agreement, conflict continued for many years in the Northwest Territory (between the Indigenous people and the settlers).

LITTLE TURTLE.

**Chief Little Turtle of the Miami tribe was one of the leaders of the alliance of Indigenous tribes that fought against the American Army.**

# REVIEW

In this lesson, you learned:

- The Northwest Territory was land given to the United States after the French and Indian war and was the first expansion west.

- The Land Ordinance of 1785 and the Northwest Ordinance of 1787 described how the territory would be divided into townships as well as created laws and explained how they could become states.

- The expansion into the Northwest Territory caused a lot of conflict between the settlers and the Indigenous people in the area. Battles over the land were fought for many years.

### Think About It
How did settlement in the Northwest Territory prepare the United States for expansion into other areas?

# PRACTICE

## Conflict From Both Sides

Conflict can be a hard thing. It is important to think about both sides of an issue when looking at a problem. Think about the conflict between the Indigenous people and the settlers in the Northwest Territory. Fill in the chart below with how each side may have been feeling or what they may have been thinking during this time. Think about how you would feel if you were one of the Indigenous people or one of the settlers.

### THOUGHTS/FEELINGS OF THE INDIGENOUS PEOPLE

### THOUGHTS/FEELINGS OF THE SETTLERS

# WHAT SHOW YOU KNOW

Decide if each statement is true or false in explaining the Land Ordinance of 1785. Circle the correct answer.

1. True or False  The land was first split into smaller territories and then into townships.

2. True or False  Each township was divided into 40 lots.

3. True or False  One lot was set aside for a public school.

4. True or False  The lots were free to the public.

5. Which of the following were rules created by the Northwest Ordinance? Circle all correct answers

A. People had to practice a certain religion.

B. No land would be taken from the Indigenous people.

C. Territories had to ask Congress to become states.

D. Public education was not allowed.

6. What laws created by the Northwest Ordinance of 1787 helped to shape some of the laws we still have today in America?

.................................................................................................................

7. What was the main conflict between the Indigenous people and the settlers? What happened as a result of this conflict?

.................................................................................................................

.................................................................................................................

# ONLINE CONNECTION

## Blue Jacket and Little Turtle

Use your computer to search for more information about Chief Blue Jacket of the Shawnees and Chief Little Turtle of the Miamis. They were the important chiefs that led the alliance of the Indigenous people in battle against the American army. What can you learn about them and their people?

# Lesson 34

## Louisiana Territory

### By the end of this lesson, you will be able to:

- identify the benefits of the Louisiana Territory purchase
- identify examples of natural resources the United States got access to when purchasing the Louisiana Territory
- trace a route down the Mississippi River on a map to show the path many people took to trade

### Lesson Review

If you need to review westward expansion, please go to the lesson titled "The Northwest Territory."

### Academic Vocabulary

Read the following vocabulary words and definitions. Look through the lesson. Can you find each vocabulary word? Underline the vocabulary word in your lesson. Write the page number of where you found each word in the blanks.

- **natural resources:** materials that people use that come from the earth (page ____)
- **port:** a place where ships can load and unload goods (page ____)

In this lesson, you will learn about the Louisiana Territory. Just like the Northwest Territory, the land eventually became different states. As you go through the lesson, see if you can figure out which 15 states were formed from the Louisiana Purchase. You can use maps to help you. Have fun exploring!

Have you ever made a deal with someone? If you have, picture that time in your mind. Maybe you are remembering how easy or difficult it was to make that deal. Do you remember feeling happy after you made your deal? Usually, both people or groups of people feel good when a deal is made. If not, then the deal probably won't happen. People also want to feel like the deal is fair.

Write about a deal that you have made. What was the deal about? Who did you make the deal with? How did you make sure the deal was fair?

..........................................................................

..........................................................................

..........................................................................

..........................................................................

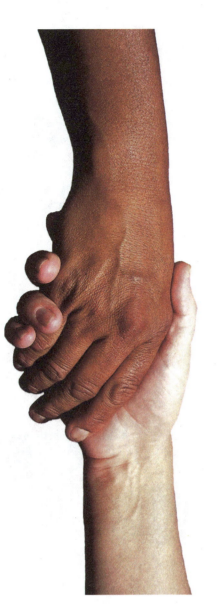

Many times, the United States has made deals with other countries to gain more land. In this lesson, you will learn how the United States continued to expand west by making a deal with France. Do you think this was an easy or hard deal to make? Why do you think the United States wanted more land?

## IN THE REAL WORLD

Talk to an adult you know about a time they made a deal with someone. Ask them questions about the deal, such as:

• What were you making a deal about?

• Was it easy or hard to make the deal?

• Why was it easy or hard to make the deal?

• What do you think makes it easy to make a deal?

# READ

## Taking Care of the Settlers

When a country does not have everything that they need, they sometimes make deals with other countries to get what they need. This is exactly what President Thomas Jefferson did in 1803.

As more and more settlers began moving to the Northwest Territory, President Thomas Jefferson wanted to make sure the settlers had everything they needed. The settlers used the Mississippi River to move goods from place to place. The river carried the goods all the way to the port of New Orleans. A **port** is a place where ships can load and unload goods. Can you imagine how important rivers and ports were for the settlers? This was the easiest and fastest way to move goods from one part of the country to another. It was also important for shipping goods to and from Europe. The settlers relied on this to make sure they had everything they needed to live on the new land.

## PURCHASING THE TERRITORY

Since the port of New Orleans was owned by France, President Jefferson sent James Monroe to France to buy the port. Monroe was surprised when Napoleon Bonaparte, the leader of France, offered to sell the entire Louisiana Territory. The United States quickly agreed to buy the land. Did you know that this one purchase doubled the size of the United States?

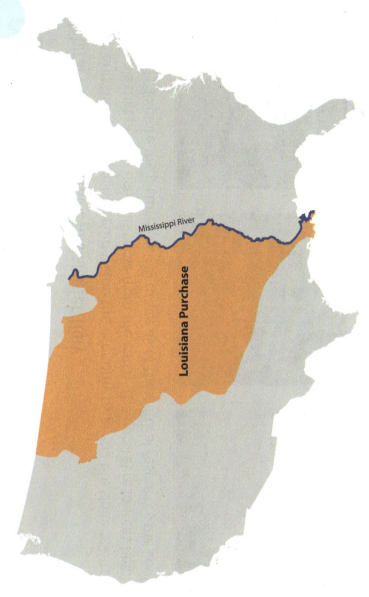

Mississippi River

**Louisiana Purchase**

The settlers of the Northwest Territory and the Louisiana Territory used the Mississippi River to trade and ship goods. New Orleans was the port city where the goods were shipped from.

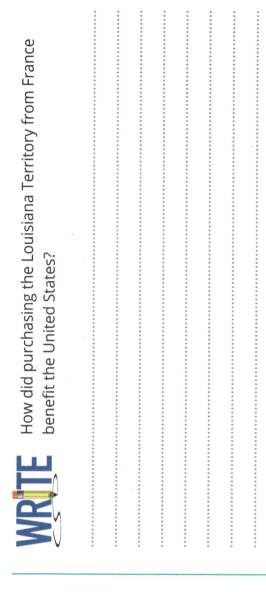

# WRITE

How did purchasing the Louisiana Territory from France benefit the United States?

...............................................................

...............................................................

...............................................................

...............................................................

...............................................................

# READ

## Natural Resources in the Louisiana Territory

The Louisiana Purchase helped develop the economy by giving the United States many more natural resources. **Natural resources** are materials that people use that come from the earth. The natural resources helped the settlers survive by providing food and building materials. Explore the pictures below to see all of the natural resources the Louisiana Territory offered the settlers.

### FRESH WATER

The settlers could use this to drink, cook, and ship goods from one place to another.

### TREES

Settlers could use the wood from the trees to build whatever they needed!

### FLAT SOIL

The area had long stretches with soil for farming.

### ANIMALS

Bison, sheep, antelope, and birds lived in the area, which were all used as food.

### MINERALS

The area was rich in minerals. Lead was used in paint. Silver was used to treat wounds. Copper was rolled into sheets for hulls of ships.

## ONLINE CONNECTION

Thomas Jefferson, James Monroe, and Napoleon Bonaparte all played important roles in helping the United States in gaining the Louisiana Territory. What else are these men famous for? Use your computer to search for more information about them. See what you can find as you explore!

# PRACTICE

## Settlers and Natural Resources

The Louisiana Territory was full of natural resources the settlers used to survive. Choose three of the natural resources you learned about. Think about how the settlers would use each natural resource. Draw a picture of the settlers using the natural resources in the Louisiana Territory. Then, write a description about your picture.

## REVIEW

In this lesson, you learned:

- President Jefferson purchased the Louisiana Territory from France. He originally wanted to buy only the port of New Orleans so the settlers could use the Mississippi River for trade. Instead, he was able to make a deal to purchase the entire Louisiana Territory and double the size of the United States!

- The Louisiana Territory was rich in natural resources. This helped the settlers so much! They were able to use the water, forests, animals, minerals, and land to help them.

### Think About It

The land that was a part of the Louisiana Territory was huge! How do you think the land that was a part of the Louisiana Territory was explored? Would you ever want to be the first person to explore new land?

# WHAT YOU SHOW KNOW

**1.** How did the Louisiana Purchase help the United States? Circle all answers that are correct.

**A.** expanded the size of the country

**B.** less fighting with the Native Americans

**C.** fewer trade partners

**D.** more natural resources

**E.** access to the Mississippi River

**2.** List two natural resources that were found in the Louisiana Territory and explain how they helped the settlers.

**1.** ............................................................

**2.** ............................................................

**3.** On the map below:

- Trace the path of the Mississippi River in blue.

- Label the area that was a part of the Louisiana Territory.

## ONLINE CONNECTION

Today, trading with other countries is still an important way the United States gets goods. Do you think trade is still done on the Mississippi River? Is New Orleans still a port city used to load and unload goods? Use an online search engine to explore and see what you can find out!

# Lesson 35

# Lewis and Clark Expedition

## By the end of this lesson, you will be able to:

- identify the importance of the Lewis and Clark Expedition
- explain the role Sacagawea played in creating relationships with Indigenous people during the Lewis and Clark Expedition
- analyze a primary source, such as a map of the Lewis and Clark Expedition
- list appropriate materials, including tools and food, that would be needed for a long expedition

## Lesson Review

If you need to review westward expansion, please go to the lesson titled "Louisiana Territory."

## Academic Vocabulary

Read the following vocabulary words and definitions. Look through the lesson. Can you find each vocabulary word? Underline the vocabulary word in your lesson. Write the page number of where you found each word in the blanks.

- **expedition:** a journey taken by a group of people with a specific purpose or goal (page ___ )
- **interpreter:** a person who translates what people are saying into other languages (page ___ )

The people you will meet in this lesson were very brave and had many decisions to make while exploring. At the end of the lesson, ask your instructor to pick one person from the lesson and role play a scene with you based on what you learned. What would their conversation be like? Think about the decisions they had to make and what they would talk about.

**A Statue of Explorers Lewis and Clark**

# EXPLORE

Imagine you were living in the early 1800s and you were asked to join the expedition and explore a new land. You will be gone for a long time, maybe years. You will be exploring land that you have never explored before. How will you get across the land? You have no idea what you will find while exploring. Maybe you will see wild animals that have never been discovered before. Or maybe you'll meet Indigenous people.

Would you go? Why or why not? Explain your thoughts and feelings on the lines below.

..............................................................................................................................................................

..............................................................................................................................................................

..............................................................................................................................................................

..............................................................................................................................................................

You have been learning all about exploring and expanding the United States. In this lesson, you will learn about a brave group of people that were the first settlers to explore the Louisiana Territory and beyond. It was a long, dangerous, and exciting journey!

## THE LEWIS AND CLARK EXPEDITION

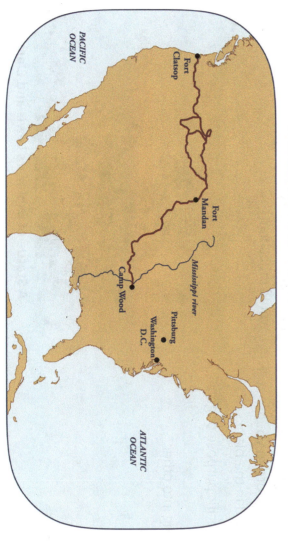

### Take A Closer Look

Study the map of the Lewis and Clark expedition. Before you begin the lesson, write down two questions you have after looking at the map. Before you read the lesson, share the questions with your instructor. As you go through the lesson, see if your questions are answered.

..............................................................

..............................................................

..............................................................

# READ

## The Lewis and Clark Expedition

President Thomas Jefferson wanted to explore the land the United States had received in the Louisiana Purchase, so he planned an expedition. An **expedition** is a journey taken by a group of people with a specific purpose or goal. Jefferson decided Meriwether Lewis would lead the expedition to explore the westward territory. Lewis asked his friend William Clark to co-lead the expedition. Lewis and Clark had both served in the US Army. Together, they gathered 45 skilled men, known as the Corps of Discovery, to help them explore.

President Jefferson had three main goals for the expedition. First, he wanted them to study and take notes on the land, plants, and animals they saw on their journey. Next, he wanted them to meet and learn about the Indigenious people who lived in the region. Finally, he wanted them to explore the Missouri and Columbia Rivers to see if they could find a water route to the Pacific Ocean.

The trek, now known as the Lewis and Clark Expedition, was one of the most important journeys in history. Throughout the expedition, they traveled by horse, boat, and on foot. Lewis and Clark made maps and kept detailed journals of the land, people, and animals they saw. They even brought back new plants and animals that had never been seen before. Can you imagine how helpful these items were? Lewis and Clark were heroes. The maps they created helped people from the Eastern United States to settle in different places across the West.

Throughout their journey, they were able to meet two of the three goals Jefferson set for them. They were not able to find a water route all the way to the Pacific Ocean, but their discoveries and interactions with the Indigenous people helped the United States to continue expanding west.

Meriwether Lewis

William Clark

# READ

## Materials Needed for a Long Expedition

Can you imagine trying to pack for a trip that you really didn't know much about? That is exactly what Lewis and Clark had to do. Here are some of the most important items they brought with them:

| ITEMS | REASONS |
|---|---|
| A Compass | To help them explore |
| Food | So they would not go hungry |
| A Spoon and Cup | To eat and drink |
| Fishing Hooks and Guns | To fish and hunt |
| Candles and Soap | To see at night and stay clean |
| Gifts for Indigenous People | To keep peace with them |

## Sacagawea

The expedition was very difficult. Luckily, Lewis and Clark met an Indigenous woman named Sacagawea who helped them on their journey. They met her at Fort Mandan just before their first winter on the expedition. Sacagawea helped them in many ways. She was a guide and also an interpreter. An **interpreter** translates what people are saying into other languages. When the expedition met Indigenous people along their journey, Sacagawea explained that their mission was peaceful.

She was also able to get horses from the Shoshone people so they could cross the Rocky Mountains. Do you think Lewis and Clark would have been able to explore all the way to the Pacific Ocean without the help of Sacagawea?

**Sacagawea with Lewis and Clark**

*Detail Lewis & Clark at Three Forks.jpg by Edgar Samuel Paxson is in the public domain.*

# WRITE

Which materials do you think were most helpful on the expedition? List three and explain why you think they were important on the lines below.

...................................................................................................................

...................................................................................................................

...................................................................................................................

...................................................................................................................

# READ

## The Route of the Expedition

On May 14, 1804, the expedition began in St. Louis, Missouri. The explorers used the Missouri River for their expedition. They had three boats. They had to travel slowly because it was a very difficult journey. Sometimes, they would have to carry their boats for miles. They traveled until it was winter. Then they had to stop and make camp. They had to wait for the snow and ice to melt. Once it was spring, they continued their journey. The expedition lasted two years, and the explorers traveled a total of 8,000 miles (12,875 kilometers). Can you imagine traveling that far and being gone for so long? What an adventure!

Study the map below. What do you notice about the route of the Lewis and Clark Expedition?

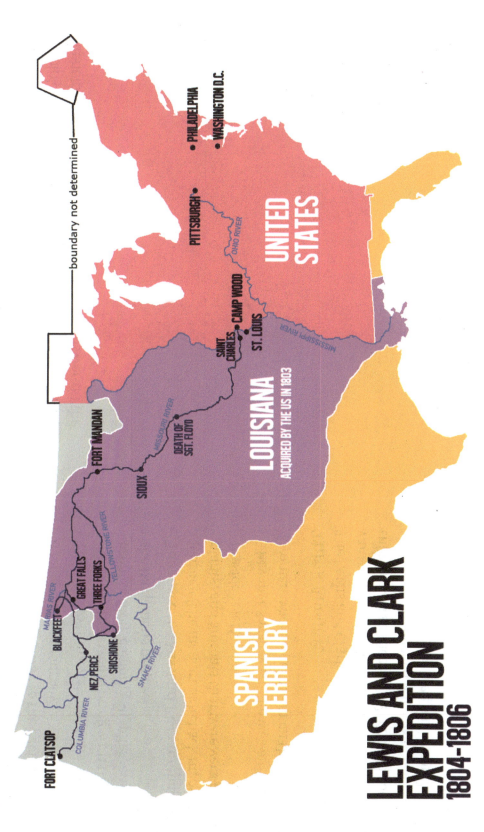

LEWIS AND CLARK EXPEDITION 1804-1806

boundary not determined

UNITED STATES

PHILADELPHIA
WASHINGTON D.C.
PITTSBURGH
OHIO RIVER

CAMP WOOD
SAINT CHARLES
ST. LOUIS
MISSISSIPPI RIVER

LOUISIANA
ACQUIRED BY THE US IN 1803

FORT MANDAN
SIOUX
MISSOURI RIVER
DEATH OF SGT. FLOYD

GREAT FALLS
THREE FORKS
YELLOWSTONE RIVER
MARIAS RIVER
BLACKFEET
NEZ PERCÉ
SHOSHONE
SNAKE RIVER
COLUMBIA RIVER
FORT CLATSOP

SPANISH TERRITORY

# PRACTICE

## The Expedition

1. Lewis and Clark met Sacagewea while at Fort Mandan. How did Sacagawea help Lewis and Clark on their journey? Write your answer on the lines below.

..................................................................

..................................................................

..................................................................

..................................................................

2. Why do you think Lewis and Clark took different routes home? Why might this be helpful to the expedition? Write your answer on the lines below.

..................................................................

..................................................................

..................................................................

..................................................................

# REVIEW

In this lesson, you learned:

- Lewis and Clark led an expedition that explored new land all the way to the Pacific Ocean. It was a long, difficult journey.

- They had to think very carefully about what materials they would bring with them. They brought food, camping supplies, and gifts for the Indigenous people.

- They used the Missouri River for much of their journey. The men brought back maps, journals, plants, and animals that were very helpful to President Jefferson.

- They met Sacagawea. She was an Indigenous woman who helped them on the expedition.

## Think About It

The Lewis and Clark Expedition took many people working together to be a success. Why do you think it was so successful? What do you think would have happened if it wasn't a success? How would that have changed our history?

# SHOW WHAT YOU KNOW

Circle all the correct answers for each question.

**1.** Why was the Lewis and Clark Expedition so important to the United States?

**A.** They made maps of the new land they explored.

**B.** They brought back new plants and animals.

**C.** They made friends with the Indigenous people.

**D.** They found a water route all the way to the Pacifc Ocean.

**2.** What tools and materials did Lewis and Clark bring on their expedition?

**A.** fishing hooks

**B.** fancy jewelry

**C.** garden tools

**D.** compass

**E.** candles

**F.** soap

**3.** Study the map to the right. Read the statements about the map, and circle all that are true.

**A.** The expedition started near St. Louis.

**B.** The expedition went past the Louisiana Territory.

**C.** Lewis and Clark stayed together for the entire expedition.

**D.** The expedition made it all the way to the Pacific Ocean.

**4.** Explain two ways Sacagawea helped on the Lewis and Clark expedition on the lines below.

................................................................

................................................................

## ONLINE CONNECTION

Sacagawea was a very important part of the Lewis and Clark expedition. Use your computer to search for more information about her. See what you can find as you explore!

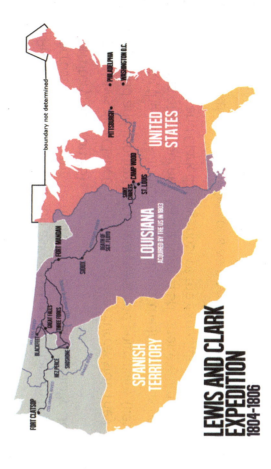

**LEWIS AND CLARK EXPEDITION**
**1804–1806**

UNITED STATES

PHILADELPHIA
WASHINGTON D.C.
PITTSBURGH
boundary not determined

SAINT CHARLES
CAMP WOOD
ST. LOUIS

FORT MANDAN

DEATH OF SGT. FLOYD

SIOUX

LOUISIANA
ACQUIRED BY THE US IN 1803

BLACKFEET
GREAT FALLS
THREE FORKS
NEZ PERCE
SHOSHONE

FORT CLATSOP

SPANISH TERRITORY

# Chapter 5 Review

**By the end of this lesson, you will:**

- review the information from the lessons in Chapter 5, "Explorations West."

## Lesson Review

Throughout the chapter, we have learned the following big ideas:

- The settlers and the Indigenous people had many conflicts during the expansion into the Northwest Territory. (Lesson 33)

- The United States expanded into the Louisiana Territory. This new territory offered new trade routes and supplied the United States with many valuable natural resources. (Lesson 34)

- President Thomas Jefferson asked Lewis and Clark to lead an expedition of men across the Louisiana Territory all the way to the Pacific Ocean to explore the new territory. (Lesson 35)

- The Lewis and Clark Expedition was very successful. They created new maps of the land and brought back new plant and animal life. (Lesson 35)

- During the Lewis and Clark Expedition, the Indigenous people were key to the success of the journey. Sacagawea, a Shoshone woman, guided and translated for Lewis and Clark during most of the expedition. (Lesson 35)

Go back and review the lessons as needed while you complete the activities.

**TAKE A CLOSER LOOK**

So much more can be learned about the Lewis and Clark Expedition. Here are pictures from the trail they traveled! Would you like to hike the Lewis and Clark trail some day? If you said yes, it would take you across 16 different states!

In Oregon, a replica of Lewis and Clark's camp setup.

Bridge along the Lewis and Clark National Historic Trail.

## The Northwest Territory

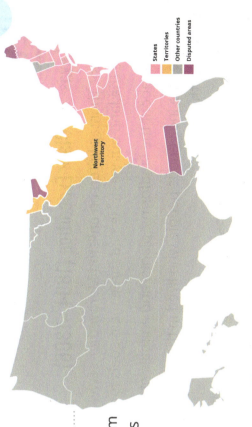

The United States took control of the Northwest Territory in 1763 after the French and Indian War. In 1785, the United States set up a standardized system where settlers could purchase titles to farmland in the undeveloped West. This was called the Land Ordinance of 1785.

The Land Ordinance outlined the process for becoming a new state and determined the government of the Northwest Territory. It also stated there needed to be public education, slavery was not allowed, and people could practice their own religion.

## SETTLERS AND THE INDIGENOUS PEOPLE

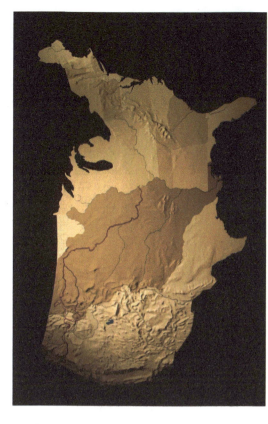

The orange shows where the Northwest Territory was located.

Settlers were not the first people to come to this region. Many Indigenous people already lived there. They were not happy their land was being taken from them and sold to new settlers. This caused many conflicts including the Northwest Indian War (1785–1795), also known as the Ohio War. The United States won the war and relocated tribes in order to make room for more settlers to come west.

## THE LOUISIANA TERRITORY

The Louisiana Territory was purchased from France by President Thomas Jefferson in 1803. He wanted to make sure the settlers in the Northwest Territory could use the Mississippi River and the port of New Orleans to ship and trade goods. The Louisiana Purchase doubled the size of the United States and provided many natural resources. The land had fresh water, minerals, forests, animals, and land to use for farming.

**Did you know the purchase of the Louisiana Territory doubled the size of the United States at the time?**

## WRITE

What was one effect of people settling westward had on the Indigenous people?

# REVIEW

## The Lewis and Clark Expedition (1804–1806)

President Thomas Jefferson enlisted Meriwether Lewis and William Clark to explore the land out west. He had three main goals for the expedition:

1. learn about the landforms, plants, and animals of the region

2. meet the Indigenous people who lived in the region and learn more about them

3. find a water route to the Pacific Ocean

The expedition started in St. Louis, Missouri, and made it all the way to the Pacific Ocean. The expedition lasted two years and the explorers traveled a total of 12874.75km. Lewis and Clark made maps and kept detailed journals of the land, people, and animals they saw.

Lewis and Clark met an Indigenous woman of the Lemhi Shoshone tribe named Sacagawea. She helped them on their journey by interpreting for them and by providing valuable knowledge of the difficult terrain. Sacagawea was a key part of the expedition's success because she was bilingual and was able to communicate with the Indigenous people of the area. She was familiar with part of the trip and guided the explorers when she knew the way.

### Sacagawea

Sacagawea was the daughter of a Shoshone chief. At age 12, she was captured by an enemy tribe and sold to a French Canadian trapper who married her. He spoke French and Hidatsa. She spoke Shoshone and Hidasta. They both joined the Lewis and Clark Expedition as valuable translators. Sacagawea was 16 at the time. She helped keep interactions between the explorers and Indigenous people peaceful.

Sacagawea carrying her son on the US dollar coin.

## WRITE

Why was Sacagawea important to the success of the Lewis and Clark expedition?

# PRACTICE

## Visualizing Vocabulary

In this chapter, you learned eight new vocabulary words: **port, natural resources, territory, ordinances, conflict, alliance, expedition,** and **interpreter.** Choose three of the vocabulary words to draw a picture of in the provided table. Next, write a sentence about your picture that includes the vocabulary word. There is an example in the first box to help you get started.

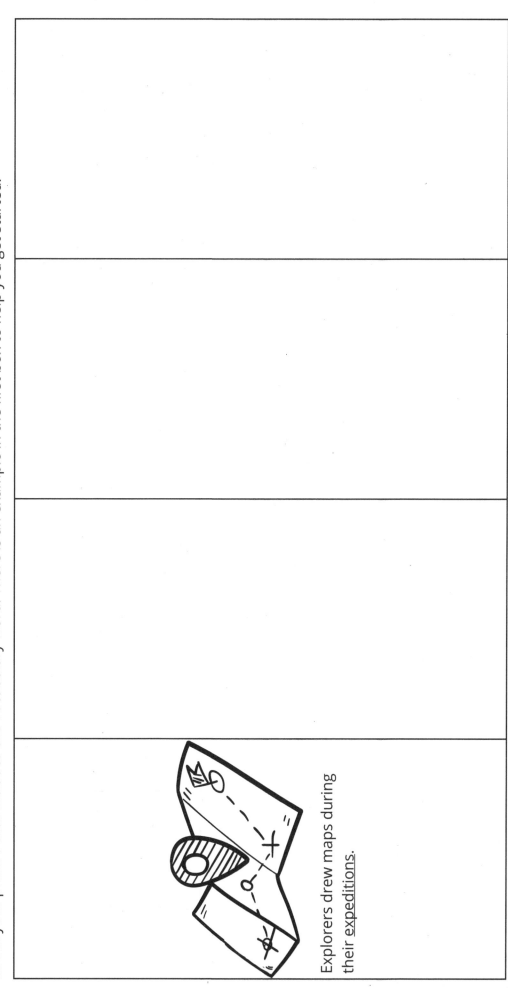

Explorers drew maps during their <u>expeditions</u>.

# PRACTICE

## Sequencing the Events of the Explorations West

Throughout the chapter, we learned about how the United States expanded westward. Read each of the events listed below. Then, write the events in the order in which they happened throughout history. Write one letter in each box. The first event should be in the first box on the left. The last event should be in the last box on the right.

A. President Thomas Jefferson asked Lewis and Clark to go on an expedition to the West.

B. The United States gained control of the Northwest Territory after the French and Indian War.

C. Lewis and Clark returned home with many helpful items including maps, new plants, and animals.

D. President Thomas Jefferson bought the Louisiana Territory from France.

E. The settlers had conflict with the Indigenous people as they moved into the Northwest Territory.

F. Lewis and Clark met Sacagawea, and she helped them on their expedition

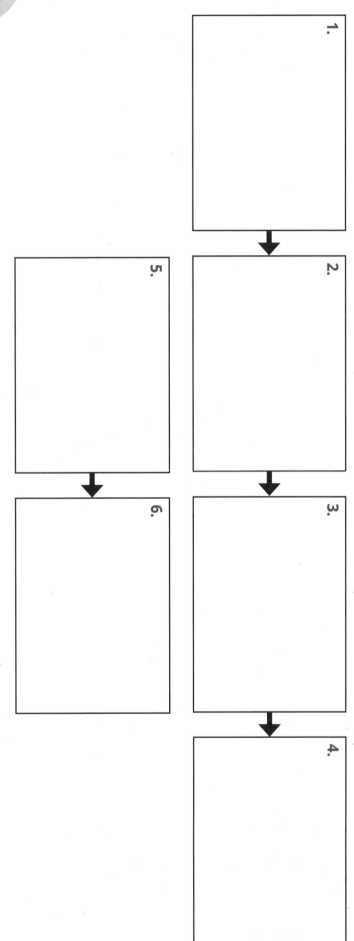

1.

2.

3.

4.

5.

6.

# PRACTICE

## Cause and Effect

Fill in the missing information in the organizer below. You will fill in either the cause or the effect of an event. The first one is already done for you to use as an example.

Remember cause and effect is the relationship between two events—one thing makes something else happen. For example, France decided to sell the Louisiana Territory (cause), so the United States bought it (effect).

| Cause | Effect |
|---|---|
| The United States gained new territory to the West after the French and Indian War and the Louisiana Purchase. | The desire to explore the West. Thomas Jefferson enlisted Lewis and Clark to lead an expedition. |
| After the Land Ordinance of 1785, new people settled where Indigenous people were already living. | |
| | Indigenous people were relocated from their native lands. |